Forms and Meanings

University of Pennsylvania Press
NEW CULTURAL STUDIES
Joan DeJean, Carroll Smith-Rosenberg,
and Peter Stallybrass, Editors

A complete listing of the books
in the series appears at the
back of this volume

Forms and Meanings

Texts, Performances, and Audiences from Codex to Computer

by Roger Chartier

University of Pennsylvania Press

Philadelphia

Library of Congress Cataloging-in-Publication Data
Chartier, Roger, 1945–
     Forms and meanings : texts, performances, and audiences from codex to
computer / by Roger Chartier.
          p.   cm. — (New cultural studies)
     Collection of four studies, two of which have been revised for
this publication with new titles, and three of which were given as
the 1994 Rosenbach lectures at the University of Pennsylvania.
     Includes bibliographical references and index.
     Contents: Representations of the written word — Princely
patronage and the economy of dedication — From court festivity to
city spectators — Popular appropriations : the readers and their books.
     ISBN 0–8122–3302–6 (cloth). — ISBN 0–8122–1546–X (pbk.)
     1. Written communication — History.   2. Transmission of texts.
3. Authors and patrons.   4. Literature and society.   5. Books and
reading.   I. Title.   II. Series.
P211.C48   1995
302.2'244'09 — dc20   95-16701
                                                                  CIP

Contents

Acknowledgments

A portion of Chapter 1 first appeared as "From Codex to Screen," translated by Laura Mason, *Common Knowledge* 3 (19): 160–71. An earlier version of Chapter 3 appeared as "George Dandin, ou le social en représentation," *Annales, Histoire, Sciences Sociales* 2 (mars-avril 1994): 277–309. An earlier version of Chapter 4 appeared as "Popular Culture: A Concept Revisited," translated by Daniel Thorburn, *Intellectual History Newsletter* 15 (1993): 3–13. Permission acknowledged to reprint these materials.

Chapters 2 and 3 and the Introduction have been translated by Lydia G. Cochrane.

I am grateful to Milad Doueihi for his help in translating the new material in Chapter 1 and to David D. Hall for his assistance with Chapter 4.

Introduction

The four studies brought together in this volume (three of which were given at the University of Pennsylvania as the 1994 Rosenbach Lectures) have very different topics, scopes, and approaches. They pose a common question, however. How are we to understand the ways in which the form that transmits a text to its readers or hearers constrains the production of meaning? The appropriation of discourse is not something that happens without rules or limits. Writing deploys strategies that are meant to produce effects, dictate a posture, and oblige the reader. It lays traps, which the reader falls into without even knowing it, because the traps are tailored to the measure of a rebel inventiveness he or she is always presumed to possess. But that inventiveness itself depends on specific skills and cultural habits that characterize all readers, inasmuch as everyone belongs to a community of interpretation. This dialectic of imposed constraint and invention occurs where conventions that put genres in a hierarchy; that codify forms; and that distinguish between discourse that is literal or figurative, historical or fabulous, demonstrative or persuasive, encounter the schemes of perception and judgment inherent to each community of readers.

Awareness of that dialectic leads to bringing into the same history everyone who contributes, each one in his or her own place and role, to the production, dissemination, and interpretation of discourse. This is the project that gives unity to this book. The two studies that make up its heart—the first dedicated to the act and the economy of the dedication, the other to the performance of a comedy on the occasion of a festive event at court—focus on the relationship between writing and political power in the age of princely patronage. Two things are important here. First, we need to grasp how dependence on royal largesse was translated into the very practice of literature. There were constraints inherent to the practice of writing—a preference shown to literary genres that lent themselves best to praise; a need to write quickly, under pressure, to satisfy the patron; a need to dispute the role of "author" with other claimants, beginning with the book-seller-printers—in a time when the market for books could not ensure economic independence and when the only recourse for authors without a title, benefice, or official post was the protection of the monarch or some other high-placed person.

Second, patronage imposed on works certain places, times, and forms of representation that governed the meanings with which they were invested. A comedy performed at court as part of a festive ritual to exalt the glory and the power of the king had meanings for the courtiers in attendance that were not identical to the meanings that the audience in Paris found in the play, or that readers who encounter the play only in a printed edition see in it. When the "same" text is apprehended through very different mechanisms of representation, it is no longer the same. Each of its forms obeys specific conventions that mold and shape the work according to the laws of that form and connect it, in differing ways, with other arts, other genres, and other texts. If we want to understand the appropriations and interpretations of a text in their full historicity we need to identify the effect, in terms of meaning, that its material forms produced.

This perspective is radically different from all approaches that hold the production of meaning to result solely from the impersonal and automatic functioning of language. When that position (which found its most blatant formulation in the "New Criticism") eliminates all individual subjectivity, considers the material forms of the inscription of discourse without significance, and abolishes any distinction between discursive and nondiscursive practices, it makes a fundamental decision to avoid all historical comprehension of works. It is a basic principle of historical comprehension to look closely, in each historical configuration, at the construction of the various categories that are manipulated for the designation, description, and classification of the various modes of discourse. This requires that we break with a universal projection of concepts and criteria — which are also inscribed in time. Among these are the notions forged at the end of the eighteenth century to describe aesthetic invention, to found literary property, or to assert the universality of judgments of taste. Restoring the variability of the categories put into play for reading and interpretation (or restoring their competitive use) requires that we take those works back to the situations that led to their production, that dictated their forms, and, for that reason, that shaped their intelligibility.

We can do this on several levels. The most ambitious (and also the riskiest) approach aims at identifying the major changes that have upset the modes of the inscription and transmission of discourse. This involves making a connection, over a very long time span, between the great revolutions of written culture: the revolution between the second and fourth centuries that changed the very structure of the book by substituting the codex for the roll; the mid-fifteenth-century revolution that invented a new way of reproducing texts and making books; the revolutions that transformed reading practices, first in the Middle Ages, then during the second half of the eighteenth century. We are not the first to raise such questions. Vico, Malesherbes, and Condorcet, for instance, saw the potential of the various writing systems, from hieroglyphs to the alphabet and then of the invention and diffusion of printing, for profoundly modifying not only conditions for the conservation and the communication of knowledge, but also the modes of the exercise and criticism of power.

Noting how variations in the form of texts affect their possible meaning can also be done on a smaller scale. One way is by deciphering different but contemporary modes of circulation and sorts of representation of a "same" work: one seventeenth-century example might be a dramatic text performed at court, presented to an urban Parisian audience, and printed, either separately or with other plays. Another way would be to follow, within a narrow time frame, successive published versions of a text or a corpus of texts available to very different publics. This is the case with the chapbooks that offered a greater number of purchasers of a humbler sort an opportunity to acquire texts that, during their original published life, reached only the restricted world of the wealthiest readers.

With the case studies and bird's-eye views presented in this book, I hope to sketch several perspectives of a more general sort. The first is a critique of some of the categories most commonly used by historians. By placing the notion of appropriation at the heart of my inquiry, I hope to demonstrate the limitations of two approaches that have long been common practice: the qualification of cultural products by the social identity of their public, and the establishment of the meaning of those products based on their linguistic function alone. Setting up an opposition between formalism and "sociologism" or between structuralist criticism and social history — a game both parties found reassuring — is no longer relevant today. The critique of the notion of "popular culture" that takes the history of publishing strategies and reading habits as its base suggests the need to shift to a point of view that recognizes social differences in contrasting customs and that holds the meanings that readers (or spectators) assign to a text to be plural and mobile.

We need to be wary of two things. The first is being too hasty to attribute a generic and univocal social qualification to cultural practices. If it is sure that there were readers (of both sexes) who belonged to the part of ancien régime society that could be called "the people," it is less sure that we can identify, in its radical specificity, a "popular" way of reading. To do so would require looking carefully at communities of readers whose principles of coherence were far from being brutally dictated by their economic condition alone, and identifying the complex of skills, conventions, and perceptions that made up the resources and the constraints by means of which they apprehended written matter. The second is setting up too rigid a dichotomy, making tactics of appropriation the only resource of powerless people who could only re-use or use for other purposes what the dominant parts of society imposed on them. Undeniably, reading is exemplary of that division of functions, because it is the construction of a meaning on the basis of a text or a book that was not produced by that reader. But what is true of reading is not necessarily true of all "popular" cultural practices. Other practices — the practices of ordinary writing offer one example — are indeed appropriations (of models, of codes, of forms, of objects), but they create a place of their own and presuppose a fixing process and a duration. They, too, were strategies. There is, therefore, no necessary connection between the social definition of appropriations and the type of practice that serves as a vehicle for them.

Another question concerns the relations between literary texts and their social world. What is involved here is the justification and the pertinence of a historical reading that, while it rejects all reduction of literary works to the status of mere historical documents (which destroys their very specificity), attempts to reconstruct their conditions of possibility and intelligibility. Such conditions are in the constraints that govern the practice of writing (for example, in constraints directly and obligatorily connected with the patronage relationship). They also involve the way in which the literary text shifts and transforms the ordinary discourse and the practices that are its matrix. This line of investigation is illustrated by the study of Molière's *George Dandin,* which poses a dual question. What social reality was represented in this comedy, and with what meanings did its different publics, at court and in the city, invest it? The answer obviously lies at the intersection of two lines of investigation: a history of the forms of the representation of the text and a reconstruction of its various receptions, and an analysis of the way that text presents the mechanisms that go into the construction of social identities. A strong connection can thus be reestablished between the circumstances that governed the writing of the play — in this case, a royal command for a festive event to celebrate the glory of the monarch — and its meaning (better, its meanings) for its seven-teenth-century spectators.

A final concern underlying this book is a reflection on our own times. How are we to situate, within the long term of history, the transformations promised and already made possible by widespread use of a new representation of the written: the electronic text that substitutes for the printed objects that trace their ancestry to the codex? To answer such a question we must do two things. First, we need to examine the changes that have begun, at an uneven rate, in the world today and place them where they belong within the revolutions in techniques for reproduction of texts, in the forms of the book, and in manners of reading. Then, taking into account the effects of meaning produced by the material aspects of writing, we need to reflect on the many consequences of our entry into the age of the electronic representation of texts and their reading on screens. These challenge all the traditional categories that have served to identify and define works; to found the concept of literary property or copyright; and to organize the practices of the description, conservation, and reading of texts. Contrary to the claims of historians in search of legitimacy, the backward glance is of little help in predicting what the future will bring. Because it is comparative, however, that backward glance can enable us to measure more accurately the changes that are revolutionizing our relations with written culture. It can also remind us that any comprehension of a text is necessarily dependent on a knowledge of the material forms it has taken. The historian's analysis is neither prophetic nor nostalgic: it has the dual task of pleading for the preservation and protection of the evidence of a written culture that for five centuries has been identified with the circulation of printed matter, and of making the revolution of the present moment more intelligible — a revolution as radical as the one that, seventeen or eighteen centuries ago, imposed a new form on the book.

1. Representations of the Written Word

I would like to open this essay by considering three eighteenth-century texts — Vico's *Scienza nuova* (1725), Condorcet's *Esquisse d'un tableau historique des progrès de l'esprit humain* (1793), and Malesherbes's *Remontrances* (1775) — each in its own manner questioning the relations between symbolic activities and the structures or modes of transmission of the oral and written. All three aim to identify the crucial moments that determine either the course of nations, the progress of the human mind, or the history of the monarchy. The method is similar in each: ages and epochs are distinguished by their characteristic forms of writing or modes of textual transmission, calling attention to the intellectual, social, or political significance of those fundamental breaks that have transformed the inscription, recording, and communication of speech.

In the Fourth Book of *New Science*, entitled "The Course Nations Run," Vico identifies three distinguishing characteristics of the three epochs — the age of gods, the age of heroes, and the age of men — that he takes over from the ancient Egyptians.[1] Each period is characterized by a particular language and writing system, intimately related, since for Vico the origin of languages and the origin of letters "were by nature conjoined" (138). The age of gods was marked by "a divine mental language [formed] by mute religious acts or divine ceremonies" (340). The hieroglyphs are the characters that express this mute language. It is one incapable of abstraction and resorts instead to objects or their representations:

> The first [characters] were divine, . . . used, as we have shown above, by all nations in their beginnings. And they were certain imaginative universals, dictated naturally by the human mind's innate property of delighting in the uniform. Since they could not achieve this by logical abstraction, they did it by imaginative representation. To these poetic universals they reduced all the particular species belonging to each genus. (341)

The second language, from the age of heroes, "was said by the Egyptians to have been spoken by symbols" (144). Composed equally of mute and articulated speech, it used signs and manipulated "metaphors, images, similitudes, or comparisons, which, having passed into articulate speech, supplied all the resources of poetic expression" (144). This language marks the first step in a process toward abstraction that reaches its conclusion with the fully articulated speech of the third language and the third species of characters, by means of which "of a hundred and twenty thousand hieroglyphic characters . . . they made a few letters" (341).

Vico describes this graphic alphabetic language as one that uses "vulgar letters," and he repeatedly discusses its origins. Rejecting opinions that credit Sanchuniathon with the discovery of the alphabet or the Egyptian Cecrops or the Phoenecian Cadmus with the introduction of alphabetic writing to Greece, he concludes that the Greeks "with supreme genius, in which they certainly surpassed all nations, took over these geometric forms to represent the various articulated sounds" (146). The invention of the alphabet marks a turning point in the evolution of civilization Vico describes. Letters are "vulgar" because they break the priestly and aristocratic monopoly over images and signs. Alphabetic writing and vulgar speech "are a right of the people" (145) and, indeed, a guarantee of liberty, "in virtue of this sovereignty over languages and letters, the free people must also be masters of their laws, for they impose on the laws the sense in which they constrain the powerful to observe them" (342).

The typology of languages and letters has a double valence. One may understand it historically as scanning the course of nations and setting the rhythm for the succession of epochs. Logically, however, this diversity of languages and writing systems must also be understood synchronically:

> "We must establish this principle: that as gods, heroes, and men began at the same time (for they were, after all, men who imagined the gods and believed their own heroic nature to be a mixture of the divine and human natures), so these three languages began at the same time, each having its letters, which developed along with it. (149)

Whether the multiplicity of languages and writing systems came sequentially or simultaneously, Vico's classification may be translated into a variety of registers.[2] In rhetorical terms, it associates a particular trope with each stage: metaphor with the hieroglyphs, which afford a way of speaking via objects or their representation; metonymy with the heroic or symbolic characters, which designate objects or beings by their particular qualities; and synecdoche with the vulgar letters or alphabetic writing, which permit the establishment of abstract categories.[3] In political terms, this classification links theocracy to divine writing, aristocratic government to heroic symbols, and popular freedom, be it republican or monarchic, to vulgar letters. In terms of knowledge, the typology of writing leads from mystical theology or the science of hieroglyphic language, to the authority of contracts, finally to the verification of facts that the alphabet makes possible. In all three cases, the most important break comes with the invention of alphabetic writing — an invention that makes abstraction possible, that institutes legality and equality, and that emancipates knowledge from the all-powerful hold of divine reason or an absolute state authority.

In the Third Epoch of his *Outlines of an Historical View of the Human Mind*, Condorcet, too, strongly emphasizes the impact of this break.[4] Only the invention of the alphabet could carry the sciences forward. The two earlier forms of writing — hieroglyphs and writing "in which conventional signs are affixed to every idea, which is the only one that the Chinese are at present acquainted with" (47) — had allowed for the confiscation and control of knowledge by the priestly and teaching castes. "The first mode of writing, which represented things by a painting more or less accurate, either of the thing itself or of an analogous object" (44), has been transformed by the priests into a secret writing that was the expression of an allegorical language. This allegorical language was invested with a meaning sacred to the people who now used another writing system "in which the resemblance of [the] objects was nearly effaced, and in which the only signs employed were in some way purely conventional" (44). Thus endowed with its own language and writing, the "secret doctrine" of the priests founded, in this state of scriptural dualism, "the most absurd creeds, the most senseless modes of worship, and the most shameful and barbarous practices. . . . All progress of the sciences was at a standstill: some even of those which had been enjoyed by preceding ages were lost to the generation that followed" (46–47).

Because alphabetic writing breaks with every form of representation, because it strips figures and signs of their mysteries, and because it takes away from the priests their monopoly over interpretation, the alphabet gives to all people "equal right to the knowledge of truth." Thus is assured "for ever the progress of the human race" (13). It is, then, not the political freedom afforded by the regime of the polis, but the introduction in Greece of a new way of representing language by "a small number of signs [that] served to express every thing" (12), that relegates the priests to a purely cultic status and that clears the way for the advancement of knowledge. In his Introduction, Condorcet delineates the stages in the progress of the human mind by outlining the different modes of knowledge possible for each epoch. Knowledge is conjectural and psychological for the first age, preceding the rise of articulated language ("We can have no other guide than an investigation of the development of our faculties"). It remains hypothetical, but founded on the collection of historical facts and anthropological observations for the second period, which ends with the invention of alphabetical writing. Knowledge becomes certain and truly historical for the third age, for "from the period in which alphabetical writing was known in Greece, history is connected by an uninterrupted series of facts and observations with the period in which we live, with the present state of mankind in the most enlightened countries of Europe, and the picture of the progress and advancement of the human mind becomes strictly historical" (14–15). Grounded in epistemology, this system of periodization is tied, as in Vico, to revolutions in the forms of communication: first the formation of articulated language, next the invention of the alphabet.[5]

Within this schema, Condorcet inscribes another revolution, bound to the invention of printing. In the Eighth Epoch of the *Esquisse,* he characterizes in three ways the effects of the invention that "multiplies indefinitely, and at a small expense, copies of any work" (120). First, where passions are excited by live exchanges in assemblies of people, the instruction that any individual can receive in silence and solitude from books encourages the cool exercise of reason, critical judgment, and rational examination of all opinions. With printing,

> a new species of tribune is established, from which are communicated impressions less lively but at the same time more solid and profound; from which is exercised over the passions an empire less tyrannical, but over reason a power more certain and durable; where all the advantage is on the side of truth, since what the art may lose in point of seduction is more than counterbalanced by the illumination [the enlightenment] it conveys. (121)

Intellect against passion, enlightenment against seduction: the second effect of printing is the substitution of evidence based on reason for beliefs drawn out by rhetorical argument. The certitude and irrefutability of the truth, conceived according to the models of logical deduction and mathematical reasoning, are thus fundamentally differentiated from the ill-founded convictions imposed and reinforced by the rhetorical art of persuasion. Finally, through printing, the truths thus established can be revealed to all. Whereas orality necessarily presupposes the fragmentation of discursive exchanges and the cloistering of knowledge, the circulation of printed texts brings with it the universal exercise of reason: "It is to the press we owe the possibility of spreading those publications which the emergency of the moment, or the transient fluctuations of opinion may require, and of interesting thereby in any question treated in a single point of view, the universality of men speaking the same language" (122). For Condorcet, then, "public opinion," so crucial to the progress of the human mind, is a creation of the printing revolution. If, in contrast to fluid, wary, locally held beliefs, public opinion is stable, certain, and universal, this is because of printing. By permitting the exchange of ideas without physical presence, by constituting a unified public out of dispersed individuals, the printing press has constructed an invisible and immaterial tribunal, whose reason-based judgments apply to everyone:

> A public opinion is formed, powerful by the number of those who share it, energetic, because the motives that determine it act upon all minds at once, though at considerable distances from each other. A tribunal is erected in favor of reason and justice, independent of all human power, from the penetration of which it is difficult to conceal any thing, from whose verdict there is no escape. (121)

The universality that printing promises remains partial and incomplete, however. Two additional conditions must be met for its full achievement. First, there must be universal "public instruction" that would break the Church's control over education and would give to everyone the necessary competence to read the books "adapted to every class of readers, and every degree of instruction" (122). Second, there must be established a common language, one capable of eliminating the contradiction implicit in a formulation such as "the universality of people who speak the same language." This universal language cannot be that of mathematics, which "necessarily divides societies into two extremely unequal classes: the one composed of men understanding the language and therefore in possession of the key to the sciences, the other of those who, incapable of learning it, find themselves reduced almost to an absolute impossibility of acquiring knowledge" (240). Condorcet refuses to construct the universal language out of scientific idiom for the same reasons that he rejects the notion of literary property: he opposes the confiscation of knowledge by a minority.[6] He concludes, consequently, that an original universal language must be created, one translatable into every vernacular tongue and capable of formalizing all acts of comprehension, logical reasoning, and rules of practice. Here, too, the forms given to the representation and diffusion of writing are paramount. This universal language uses signs to express "either the direct objects, or these well-defined collections constituted of simple and general ideas, which are to be found or may be introduced equally in the understandings of all mankind; or lastly, the general relations of these ideas, the operations of the human mind, the operations peculiar to any science, and the mode of process in the arts" (239). Its full effectiveness relies upon recourse to what Condorcet designates "technical methods"—in fact, the material bases for cognitive operations. Thus, for example, tables and charts, made easier and more available by printing, enable the reader to grasp the relations and combinations that link facts, objects, numbers, and formulas. The limitless perfectibility of humankind, promised and made possible by the universal language that will endow each field of knowledge with the certainty of mathematics, is thus closely bound up with the technical invention that alone could bring the possibilities opened by alphabetical writing to their final and most beneficial fulfillment.

In his *Remontrances*, written in 1775 in the name of the Cour des Aides, a sovereign court of which he was the First President, Malesherbes also insists on the fundamental shift brought about by the invention of printing.[7] In this text, the purpose of which is to denounce the despotic tendencies of the monarchy, Malesherbes looks to history to make a case for the necessary return to the "primitive constitution of monarchy" (272). The secretiveness of the workings of government and the stifling of all public complaint—the characteristics, that is, of despotism—find their origins in the nation's past. Malesherbes divides this past into three ages, but as his object is not the progress of civilization but national history, his periodization does not correspond exactly to the one Condorcet would propose twenty years later.

Although writing was already known in the first age, the "time of our first ancestors," it was not yet invested with judicial and administrative authority. These resided entirely in speech. Hence the public authority of judicial decisions orally delivered by the king in front of the assembled nation in the Champ de Mars, or by the nobles, "each in his own domain," hearing the petitions of plaintiffs and gathering the opinions of those present. Hence, too, the instability, uncertainty, and variability of the law. This age of "verbal conventions" is succeeded by the "age of writing," in which law is fixed, jurisprudence made exact, and the rights of citizens established on the basis of common principles. This evolution comes at a high price, however, as a double secrecy is installed: the secrecy of administration, henceforth separated from justice, and the secrecy of judicial procedures now based on written documents. The usurpation of justice by a "new order of citizens," the magistrates, corresponds to the secretiveness of an administration that acts through the king's written orders instead of public proclamations. Far from fortifying the public freedom proper to a monarchy, the judicial and administrative use of writing planted the seeds of despotic corruption (270–72).

This secrecy is all the more intolerable in that it survives into a subsequent age. The age of printing is, in effect, the era in which "the art of printing has multiplied the advantages that writing has given to men, and has abolished its shortcomings." The public nature of petitions, deliberations, and decisions is no longer incompatible with the firm establishment and stability of law. As will be the case with Condorcet, the printed word, which allows for detached and reflexive reading, quiets the enthusiasms and passions that can take over a "tumultuous assembly." And as in Condorcet, the printed word provides the very foundation for the formation of a sovereign public: "the judges themselves may be judged by an informed Public." It is in the name of this public that the assembled representatives of the nation, that is, the Estates General, should be able to examine, discuss, and criticize the acts of the royal administration. But as the king has not yet decided to convene the Estates General, this task of representation is delegated to substitutes: on the one hand, to the sovereign courts, on the other to men of letters. In the new public space created by the circulation of the printed word, these men of letters stand in for "those who, endowed with a natural eloquence, were listened to by our fathers in the Champ de Mars or in the public trials" (272–73).

Several months earlier, in January 1775, Malesherbes had developed a similar idea in his inaugural speech for the Académie Française. There, he asserted the full sovereignty of the public erected as a supreme tribunal:

> The Public is avidly curious about objects about which it was formerly indifferent. It is created into a Tribunal independent of all powers and that all powers respect; it appreciates all talents and recognizes all merit. And in an enlightened century in which every citizen can speak to the entire nation in print, those who have the talent to move and instruct, that is to say, those Men of Letters, are to a dispersed public what the orators of Rome and Athens were to an assembled public. This truth that I expose in front of the assembly of the Men of Letters has already been presented to certain Magistrates, and none refused to recognize the tribunal of the Public as the sovereign judge of all judges of the Earth.

Malesherbes thus formulates the notion that the judgments of the public — a public that exists only because of the circulation of the printed word — guides the opinions of all other judges, including the king, "certain never to err in his judgments because he judges only on the basis of the infallible testimony of an enlightened nation," the magistrates charged with upholding the rule of law, or the academicians, celebrated by Malesherbes as "the supreme Judges of Literature."[8] Like the lawyers and public representatives of the *Remontrances*, the Men of Letters (or at least their *sanior pars*) are here invested with a true public office and are endowed with a judicial competence that was, during the ancien régime, the basis of all authority. Opposed, as in Condorcet, to the age of orality, print culture redefines the exercise of power, social roles, and intellectual practices.

By organizing large-scale periodization according to the mutations of the forms of inscription, transmission, and recording of discourse, Vico, Condorcet, and Malesherbes inaugurate in the eighteenth century a set of reflections that continue today in the works of Walter Ong,[9] Jack Goody,[10] and Henri-Jean Martin.[11] All three identify the major transformations that overturn the modes of textual circulation and transmission. It is in this context that I would inscribe this essay.

*　　*　　*

"Books no longer exercise the power they once did; in the face of the new means of information and communication to which we will have access in the future, books will no longer master our reason and our feelings."[12] This remark by Henri-Jean Martin will serve as the point of departure for these reflections. They are meant to locate and designate the effects of a revolution that is dreaded by some and applauded by others, asserted as ineluctable or simply believed possible: in short, the radical transformation of the modes of production, transmission, and reception of the written word. Dissociated from the forms in which we are used to encountering them (books, newspapers, periodicals), texts will henceforth be destined for an electronic existence; composed on the computer or digitalized, conveyed by electronic processes, they will reach the reader on screen in a machine-readable form.

I have, myself, a dual perspective on this future (which may already be a present), in which texts are detached from the form of the book that emerged in the West seventeen or eighteen centuries ago. One perspective is that of a historian of written culture who is primarily concerned with uniting in a single history the study of texts (canonical or ordinary, literary or common) with the conditions of their transmission and dissemination, their readers, their uses, and their interpretations. A second perspective is linked to the fact that I was a participant (to a modest degree) in the project of the Bibliothèque de France, of which one of the essential axes is the constitution of a major corpus of electronic texts that can be transmitted over great distances and that may become the object of a new kind of reading, made possible through a computer-assisted reading post.

My first question, asked from both these points of view, is, How do we situate within the long history of the book, of reading, and of relations to the written word, the revolution that has been predicted, has in fact already begun, which transforms the book (or the written object) as we know it — with its quires, its leaves, its pages — into an electronic text to be read on a screen? Answering this question requires drawing sharp distinctions among three kinds of transformations, the relations among which are still unclear. The first revolution was technical: in the mid-fifteenth century it completely changed the means of reproducing texts and producing books. With the introduction of movable type and the printing press, manuscript copies ceased to be the only available means for the multiplication and circulation of texts. Hence the stress that has been placed on this critical moment in Western history, which is said to mark "the appearance of the book" and to be a "revolution."[13]

In recent years, the emphasis has shifted somewhat, to stress the limits of this first revolution. It is now clear that Gutenberg's invention did not alter the essential structures of the book. Until at least the beginning of the sixteenth century, the printed book remained very much dependent on the manuscript. It imitated its predecessor's layout, scripts, and appearance, and, above all, it was completed by hand: the hand of the illuminator who painted ornamented or historiated initials or miniatures; the hand of the corrector or *emendator*, who added punctuation, rubrics, and titles; the hand of the reader who inscribed notes and marginalia on the page.[14] More fundamentally, after Gutenberg as before, the book continued to be an object composed of folded sheets, gathered between covers and bound together. The Western book achieved the form it would retain in print culture twelve or thirteen centuries before the introduction of the new technology.

A look East offers a second reason to reevaluate the print revolution. Study of China, Korea, and Japan reveals that techniques proper to the West were not the necessary condition, for those Asian cultures possessed not only writing but widespread printing.[15] Movable type was known in the East; it was invented and used there well before Gutenberg's time; terra cotta characters were used in China in the eleventh century, and texts were printed with metallic characters in thirteenth-century Korea. The use of movable type in the East unlike the post-Gutenberg Occident, remained, however, limited and discontinuous, monopolized by emperor and monasteries. But this does not imply the absence of a large-scale print culture. That was made possible by another technique: xylography, or the engraving of texts on wood, which were then printed by rubbing them. Xylography, documented in Korea after the mid-eighth century and in China from the late ninth century, introduced to Ming and Qing China and Tukogawa Japan the broad circulation of print, commercial publishing enterprises independent of the state, a dense network of libraries and reading societies, and broadly diffused popular genres.

It is not, therefore, necessary to measure the print culture of Eastern civilizations solely by the standards of Western techniques, as though by default. Xylography has its particular advantages. It is better adapted than movable type to languages that possess a large number of characters or, as in Japan, a plurality of scripts; it sustains a powerful association between handwriting and print, because the wood is engraved from calligraphic models; and, because of the durability of well-conserved wood, it permits the adjustment of print runs according to demand. Such considerations should lead us to a more balanced appreciation of Gutenberg's invention. Undeniably fundamental, it is not the only technology capable of ensuring the broad dissemination of the printed book.

Our current revolution is obviously more extensive than Gutenberg's. It modifies not only the technology for reproduction of the text, but even the materiality of the object that communicates the text to readers. Until now, the printed book has been heir to the manuscript in its organization by leaves and pages, its hierarchy of formats (from the *libro da banco* to the *libellus*), and its aids to reading (concordances, indices, tables).[16] The substitution of screen for codex is a far more radical transformation because it changes methods of organization, structure, consultation, even the appearance of the written word. Such a revolution requires other terms of comparison.

The long-term history of reading provides us with the essentials. Two fundamental changes organize its chronology. The first accents a transformation of the physical and corporal modes of the act of reading and stresses the decisive importance of a shift from necessarily oralized reading, indispensable for the reader's comprehension, to reading that may be silent and visual.[17] This revolution took place during the long Middle Ages, as silent reading, initially restricted (between the seventh and ninth centuries) to monastic scriptoria, spread to the world of schools and universities (by the twelfth century) and then to lay aristocrats (two centuries later). Its precondition was the separation of words by Irish and Anglo-Saxon scribes during the high Middle Ages, and its consequences were considerable, creating the possibility of reading more quickly, and so reading more texts and more complex texts.

This perspective evokes two observations. First, simply because the medieval West learned to read visually and in silence, we need not assume that ancient Greeks and Romans were unable to do so. The absence of separations between words did not prohibit silent reading in antique civilizations among populations for whom written and vernacular languages were the same.[18] The practice, common among the ancients, of reading aloud, for others or for oneself, should not be attributed to an inability to read with the eyes alone (which was practiced in the Greek world from the sixth century before Christ),[19] but to a cultural convention that powerfully associated text and voice, reading, declamation, and listening.[20] Moreover, oralized reading persisted into the modern period when silent reading had already become an ordinary practice for educated readers, between the sixteenth and eighteenth centuries. At that time, reading aloud remained the fundamental cement of diverse forms of sociability — familial, learned, worldly, or public — and the reader envisioned by numerous literary genres was one who read or listened to others. In Golden Age Castile, *leer* and *oír*, *ver* and *escuchar* were quasi-synonymous, and reading aloud was the implied reading of very different genres: all the poetic genres, the humanist comedy (consider the *Celestina*), the novel in all its forms until *Don Quixote*, even history itself.[21]

The second observation takes the form of a question: Should we not place greater stress on the role of the written word than on ways of reading? If such is the case, then the twelfth century marks a critical rupture, for then writing ceased to be strictly a means of conservation and memorization and came to be composed and copied for reading that was understood as intellectual work. In schools and universities, the monastic model of writing was succeeded by the scholastic one. In monasteries, books were not copied to be read. Rather, they hoarded knowledge as the patrimonial wealth of the community and sustained uses that were, above all, religious (the *ruminatio* of a text that was truly incorporated by the faithful, meditation, prayer). Urban schools changed everything: the place of book production, which passed from scriptorium to stationer's shop; the book's forms, in the multiplication of abbreviations, marks, glosses, and commentaries; and even the method of reading, which ceased to be participation in the mystery of the Sacred Word, and became a regulated and hierarchized decoding of the letter (*littera*), the sense (*sensus*), and the doctrine (*sententia*).[22] Thus the accomplishment of silent reading cannot be separated from the enormous change that transformed the very function of writing.

Another "revolution in reading" concerns the style of reading. In the second half of the eighteenth century, "intensive" reading was succeeded by what has been described as "extensive" reading.[23] The "intensive" reader faced a narrow and finite body of texts, which were read and reread, memorized and recited, heard and known by heart, transmitted from generation to generation. Religious texts, and above all the Bible in Protestant countries, were the privileged sustenance of such reading, which was powerfully imbued with sacredness and authority. The "extensive" reader, that of the *Lesewut,* the rage for reading that overtook Germany in Goethe's time, is an altogether different reader — one who consumes numerous and diverse print texts, reading them with rapidity and avidity and exercising a critical activity over them that spares no domain from methodical doubt.

This view is open to discussion. There were, in fact, many "extensive" readers during the period of the supposed "intensive" reading: consider the humanists who accumulated readings to create their commonplace books.[24] The inverse case is truer still: it was at the very moment of the "reading revolution" that the most "intensive" readings developed (with Rousseau, Goethe, and Richardson), readings in which the novel seized its readers to become a part of them and to govern them as the religious text had once done.[25] Moreover, for the most numerous and most humble readers — those of chapbooks, the *Bibliothèque bleue*, or the *literatura de cordel* — reading long remained a rare and difficult practice. It was based on the memorization and recitation of texts that became familiar because they were so few, of texts that were, in fact, recognized more than discovered.

These necessary precautions, which moderate an overly stark opposition between two styles of reading, do not, however, invalidate the proposition that a "reading revolution" took place in the second half of the eighteenth century. Its forms were readily apparent in England, Germany, and France: the expansion of book production, the multiplication and transformation of newspapers, the success of small formats, the fall of book prices (thanks to pirated editions), and the expansion of reading societies (book clubs, *Lesegesellschaften, chambres de lecture*) and lending libraries (circulating libraries, *Leihbibliotheken, cabinets de lecture*). Described as a danger to the political order, as a narcotic (Fichte's word), or as a disordering of the imagination and the senses, this "rage for reading" profoundly impressed contemporary observers. There is no doubt that it played an essential role in the critical distancing that alienated subjects from their monarch and Christians from their church throughout Europe and especially in France.

The revolution of the electronic text will also be a revolution in reading. To read on a screen is not to read in a codex. The electronic representation of texts completely changes the text's status; for the materiality of the book, it substitutes the immateriality of texts without a unique location; against the relations of contiguity established in the print objects, it opposes the free composition of infinitely manipulable fragments; in place of the immediate apprehension of the whole work, made visible by the object that embodies it, it introduces a lengthy navigation in textual archipelagos that have neither shores nor borders.[26] Such changes inevitably, imperatively require new ways of reading, new relationships to the written word, new intellectual techniques. While earlier revolutions in reading took place without changing the fundamental structure of the book, such will not be the case in our own world. The revolution that has begun is, above all, a revolution in the media and forms that transmit the written word. In this sense, the present revolution has only one precedent in the West: the substitution of the codex for the *volumen* — of the book composed of quires for the book in the form of a roll — during the first centuries of the Christian era.

This earliest revolution, which invented the book as we still know it, raises three questions.

First is that of its date.[27] The available archaeological evidence, furnished by excavations in Egypt, permits several conclusions. On the one hand, the roll was earliest and most effectively replaced by the codex in Christian communities: from the second century, all recovered manuscripts of the Bible take the form of a codex written on papyrus, while 90 percent of the biblical texts and 70 percent of the liturgical and hagiographic texts we possess from the second through fourth centuries are also in the form of the codex. On the other hand, there was a significant lag before Greek literary and scientific texts adopted the new form of the book. It was not until the third and fourth centuries that the number of codices for Greek texts equaled that of rolls. Even if the dating of biblical texts on papyrus is debatable, sometimes moved up to the third century, preference for the codex remains powerfully associated with Christianity.

The second question concerns the reasons for the adoption of this new form of book. The classic explanations remain pertinent, even if they must be nuanced. The use of both sides of the page undoubtedly reduced the cost of producing a book, but it was not accompanied by other possible econo-mies, such as reduction in the size of script and narrowing of margins. Moreover, although the codex demonstrably permits the joining of a large number of texts into a smaller volume, this advantage was not immediately exploited. During the first centuries of its existence, the codex remained of modest size, composed of fewer than one hundred fifty sheets — about three hundred pages. (It was not until the beginning of the fourth or even the fifth century that the codex expanded to incorporate the content of several rolls.) Finally, the codex undeniably facilitates organization and handling of the text. It permits pagination, the creation of indexes and concordances, and the comparison of one passage with another; better yet, it permits a reader to traverse an entire book by paging through. From this set of advantages followed the adaptation of the new form of the book to the textual needs of Christianity: in particular, comparing the Gospels and mobilizing citations of the Sacred Word for preaching, worship, and prayer. Beyond Christian circles, however, mastery and use of the possibilities of the codex gained ground only slowly. It appears to have been adopted by readers who were not part of the educated elite — which remained hardily faithful to Greek models, hence to the *volumen* — and initially it was texts outside the literary canon (such as scholarly texts, technical works, and novels) that were put in codex form.

Among the consequences of the shift from roll to codex, two in par-ticular merit special attention. First, while the codex imposed its form, it did not render obsolete former designations or representations of the book. In Augustine's *City of God*, for example, the term *codex* designates the book as physical object, but *liber* is used to mark divisions within the work. Thus is preserved the memory of the ancient form — "book" here becomes a unit of discourse corresponding to the quantity of text held by a single roll (the *City of God* is composed of twenty-two books).[28] In the same way, the representation of books on money and monuments, in painting and sculp-ture, remained firmly attached to the *volumen*, the symbol of knowledge and authority even after the codex had imposed its new materiality and required the acquisition of new reading practices. Furthermore, to be read — in other words, unrolled — the roll had to be held with two hands. Thus, as frescos and bas-reliefs illustrate, the impossibility of a reader's writing and reading at the same time, and thus, too, the importance of dictation. The reader was liberated by the codex. Resting on a table or lectern, the book in quires no longer required participation of so much of the body. One might thus distance oneself, reading and writing at the same time, moving at one's own pace from page to page, from book to book. With the codex as well came the invention of a formal typology that associated formats and genres, types of books and categories of discourse, so initiating a grid for identifying and categorizing books that the printing press would inherit and that we still possess today.[29]

Why this backward glance? Why, in particular, pay so much attention to the birth of the codex? Because understanding and mastering the electronic revolution of tomorrow (or today) very much depends on properly situating it within history over the *longue durée*. This permits us fully to appreciate the new possibilities created by the digitalization of texts, their electronic transmission, and their reception by computer. In the world of electronic texts, or, more appropriately, of the electronic representation of texts, two constraints that have been considered insurmountable until now may be eliminated. The first constraint is that which narrowly limits the reader's interaction with the text. Since the sixteenth century — in other words, since printers took charge of the signs, marks, and chapter or running titles that were added manually to the printed page by the reader-emendator or book owner in the time of incunabula — the reader can only insinuate his or her own writing in the virgin spaces of the book. The printed object imposes its form, structure, and layout without in any way presupposing the reader's participation. A reader who nevertheless intends to inscribe his or her presence in the object can do so only by surreptitiously, clandestinely occupying the spaces in the book that have been left free of printing: interiors of covers, blank pages, margins of the text.[30]

With the electronic text, matters will never again be the same. The reader can not only subject an electronic text to numerous processes (index it, annotate it, copy it, disassemble it, recompose it, move it), but, better yet, become its coauthor. The distinction that is highly visible in the printed book between writing and reading, between the author of the text and the reader of the book, will disappear in the face of an altogether different reality: one in which the reader becomes an actor of multivocal composition or, at the very least, is in a position to create new texts from fragments that have been freely spliced and reassembled. Like the manuscript reader who could join extremely diverse works in a single book, uniting them at will with a single binding in the same *libro-zibaldone*, the reader in the electronic age can construct collections of original texts whose existence and organization depend on the reader alone. But, more important, one can intervene in those texts at any moment, modifying them, rewriting them, making them one's own. We can see how such possibilities call into question and imperil the categories we use to describe literary works, which have been associated since the eighteenth century with an individual, singular, and original creative act and on which are founded the very concept of literary property. The idea of copyright, understood as an author's right of property over an original work that is the product of his or her creative genius (the term was first used in 1701),[31] is ill-suited to the means of composition afforded by electronic databases.[32]

On the other hand, the electronic text makes it possible for the first time to overcome a contradiction that has long haunted the West. That contradiction opposes the dream of a universal library (which brings together all books ever published; all texts ever written; indeed, as Borges suggested, all books that could possibly be written, exhausting every combination of letters of the alphabet) against the necessarily disappointing reality of collections that, no matter how large, can provide only a partial, lacunary, and mutilated image of universal knowledge.[33] The West has created an exemplary and mythic figure of this nostalgia for lost exhaustiveness: the library of Alexandria.[34] The communication of texts over distances annuls the heretofore insoluble distinction between the place of the text and the place of the reader, and so makes this ancient dream possible, accessible. The text in its electronic representation can reach any reader endowed with the necessary means to receive it. If all existing texts, manuscript or printed, were digitalized (in other words, converted into electronic text), then the universal availability of the written inheritance would become possible. All readers, wherever they might be, with the sole condition that it be before a reading post connected to a network for the distribution of computerized documents, could consult, read, study any text, regardless of its original location.[35] "When it was proclaimed the library contained all books, the first impression was one of extravagant happiness": the extravagant happiness of which Borges spoke is promised us by the libraries without walls, even without specific location, that are undoubtedly in our future.[36]

Extravagant happiness — but perhaps not without risk. In fact, each form, each medium, each structure for the transmission and reception of the written word profoundly affects its possible uses and interpretations. In recent years, historians of the book have attempted to discern, at various levels, the implications of these forms.[37] Examples abound of the ways in which transformations of material typography (in the broadest sense of the word) have profoundly changed the uses, circulation, and understanding of the "same" text:

- The variations in divisions of the biblical text, in particular those derived from the editions of Robert Estienne with their numbered verses.
- The imposition of devices proper to printed books (title and title page, woodcuts, division into chapters) onto works that were wholly foreign to print culture because their initial form was tied to a uniquely manuscript circulation. Such was the case, for instance, of the *Lazarillo de Tormes*, an apocryphal letter without title, chapters, or illustrations, which was intended for a literate public and was transformed by its first publishers into a book similar in presentation to a life of the saints or *relación de sucesos* — in other words, into one of the most widely circulated genres of Golden Age Spain.[38]
- The transformation, in England, of theatrical works from Elizabethan editions, which were rudimentary and compact, into editions that, in adopting classical French conventions at the beginning of the eighteenth century, made divisions between acts and scenes and restored some theatrical action to the printed text by including information about the stage directions.[39]
- The colportage editions of already published, mostly learned texts, requiring new forms in order to reach more "popular" readers in Castile, England, and France.

These cases are parallel. The significance, or better yet, the historically and socially distinct significations, of a text, whatever they may be, are inseparable from the material conditions and physical forms that make the text available to readers.

From these cases we may draw a powerful lesson for the present: the transfer of a written heritage from one medium to another, from the codex to the screen, would create immeasurable possibilities, but it would also do violence to the texts by separating them from the original physical forms in which they appeared and which helped to constitute their historical significance. Imagine that, in a more or less distant future, the works of our tradition could be communicated or understood only via electronic representation. There would be an enormous risk of losing the intelligibility of a textual culture in which there was a long-standing and crucial association between the idea of the text and a particular form of the book: the codes. Nothing better demonstrates the power of this association than the traditional Western metaphors that represent the book as a figure for destiny, the cosmos, or the human body.[40] From Dante to Shakespeare, from Raymond Lull to Galileo, the book used metaphorically was not *any* book: it was composed of quires, constituted by leaves and pages, protected by binding. The metaphor of the Book of the World, the Book of Nature, which has been so powerful in the early modern era, is secured by immediate and deeply rooted representations that associate the written word with the codex. The universe of electronic texts necessarily signifies a distancing from the mental representations and intellectual operations that are specifically tied to the form that the book has taken in the West for seventeen or eighteen centuries. In truth, no "order of discourse" is separable from the "order of books" with which it is contemporaneous.

Thus it seems to me imperative to elaborate two requirements. On the one hand, the profound transformation that is currently altering all modes of communication and reception of the written word must be accompanied by historical, juridical, and philosophical reflection. A technical revolution cannot be simply ignored or reacted to. The codex actually overcame and supplanted the roll, even if the latter persisted throughout the Middle Ages in another form (the scroll) destined for other uses (in particular, archival). Printing replaced manuscript, overwhelmingly, as a means for reproducing and disseminating texts, even if copying by hand continued to play its part in the circulation of numerous genres of texts — those produced according to the aristocratic and literary model of the Gentleman Writer, or those produced by entrepreneurial shops, or those circulating in "scribal communities" that were bound by secrets, friendship, or intellectual complicity.[41] One may suppose that in the twenty-fifth century, in that 2440 that Louis-Sebastien Mercier imagined in his utopia, the Library of the King (or of France) will not be a "little office" that holds only tiny volumes in duodecimo that concentrate all useful knowledge,[42] but will be a single point in a network stretching across the entire planet, ensuring the universal accessibility of a textual inheritance available everywhere thanks to its electronic form. The moment has thus come better to designate and understand the effects of such a transformation. Considering that texts are not necessarily books (or even periodicals or newspapers, which also derive from the codex), the time has also come to redefine the juridical notions (literary property, author's rights, copyright), administrative regulations and institutions (*dépôt légal*, national library), and library practices (cataloguing, classification, bibliographical description) that have been conceived and understood in relation to another form of production, conservation, and communication of the written word.

But we face a second requirement, indissolubly linked to the first. The library of the future must also be a place that will preserve the knowledge and understanding of written culture in the forms that were, and still are today, very much its own. The electronic representation of all texts whose existence did not begin with computerization should not in any way imply the relegation, forgetting, or, worse yet, destruction of the objects in which they were originally embodied. More than ever, perhaps, one of the critical tasks of the great libraries is to collect, to protect, to inventory (for example, in the form of collective national catalogues, the first step toward retrospective national bibliographies), and, finally, to make accessible the kinds of books that have been those of men and women who have read since the first centuries of the Christian era, the kinds of books that are still our own. Only by preserving the understanding of our culture of the codex may we wholeheartedly realize the "extravagant happiness" promised by the screen.

2. Princely Patronage and the Economy of Dedication

In *The Tempest,* which was performed at court on 1 November 1611 before James I, Shakespeare presented a prince who, to his misfortune, preferred the company of books to the art of government. Prospero, the duke of Milan, had given up the exercise of power in order to devote all his time to the study of the liberal arts and secret knowledge. "Being transported and rapt in secret studies," his only aspiration had been to flee the world and find refuge in his library: "Me, poor man, my library was dukedom large enough" (1.2.109–10).[1] Prospero had given over the business of governing the state to his brother Antonio. This primary disruption of normal order was the source of all the troubles. It was reflected on the political level when Antonio betrayed his trust, proclaimed himself duke, and banished Prospero from his own dukedom, and on the cosmic level by the storm of the opening scene that turns the order of Nature upside down just as Antonio's usurpation of power had destroyed political order. The story told in *The Tempest* is one of reconciliation. At the end of the play, the harmony that had been broken is fully restored, thus mending the initial rupture that had made Prospero an all-powerful magician, the master of the elements and the spirits, but also a penniless sovereign stripped of his throne, banished, and living in exile on an uncharted isle.[2]

The mirror the play offered the living prince reflected both the power of books and their danger. It is thanks to the books the faithful Gonzalo enabled Prospero to take with him in the ship that bore him away ("Knowing I loved my books, he furnish'd me / From mine own library with volumes that / I prize above my dukedom"; 1.2.166–68) that Prospero can loose the fury of the waves or calm them, call up spirits, and cast spells to enchant human beings. But it was that same limitless passion for books — in particular, for books of hidden knowledge — that made him lose his throne. The restoration of legitimate sovereignty and the reestablishment of political order thus require that he renounce the books that give power only at such a high price: "But this rough magic / I here abjure. . . . I'll break my staff, / Bury it certain fathoms in the earth, / And deeper than did ever plummet sound / I'll drown my book"; 5.1.50–57).[3]

Prospero's library is personal and "secret": it was the library of a prince, but that does not make it a princely library in the sense of a collection brought together for a sovereign but not necessarily for his personal use. We need to make this distinction clear from the outset: the "king's library" should not be too hastily equated with the king's books, and even less with what the king read. This distinction can be illustrated in exemplary fashion in France: after the 1570s the king's "library" — *la librairie du roi* — was removed from the Château de Fontainebleau and transported to Paris, where it was housed in buildings that were not royal residences — at first in a private house, in 1594 in the Collège de Clermont, in 1603 in the Couvent des Cordeliers, in 1622 in a building on the rue de la Harpe but still within the walls of the Cordeliers' friary, and in 1666 in two houses Colbert and his brother had bought on the rue Vivienne. The royal collection remained there until 1721, when it was installed in the Hôtel de Nevers. From the last third of the sixteenth century on, the "Bibliothèque du Roy" (the term first appeared in an edict of 1618) did not occupy a building that was also the ruler's residence. The king's own books — the ones that he himself read and that formed the Cabinet du Louvre — were not mingled with the books that made up the more "public" collection of the royal library. One proof of this separation is a rule established in 1658 requiring bookseller-printers to add a fifth copy of all books published to those they already deposited with governmental authorities. Two of these copies went into the Bibliothèque du Roi, one went to the Communauté des Libraires-Imprimeurs (the book trade's professional guild), one went to the Chancellor, and the fifth went to the library at the Louvre "ordinarily called the *Cabinet des Livres* [books] that serve our person."[4] Outside the Louvre, when the king went to his various other palaces and houses he had in them or carried with him the books he most enjoyed.

This had been the standard procedure for French kings even before the royal library was moved from Fontainebleau to Paris. In an inventory drawn up in 1518 of the books in the king's library in the Château de Blois there is a heading "Other books that the King commonly carries" that lists seventeen works to be put into the chests that followed the king as he moved from place to place.[5] It was not for personal reasons that François I created a new royal library at Fontainebleau around 1520; then, in 1537, made it obligatory to deposit of a copy of all the "works worthy of being seen" in the library at Blois; and, finally, brought the two libraries together at Fontainebleau in 1544. These collections had a totally "public" purpose: they were intended as places for the conservation of books and as a means for protecting all meritorious books from falling into oblivion. They were open to scholars and men of learning: as Robert Estienne wrote concerning the library at Fontainebleau, "Our king . . . offers it freely to whoever has need of it."[6] Moreover, public use was one of the arguments advanced for transferring the *librairie* to the capital. In 1567, Pierre de la Ramée (Petrus Ramus) reminded Catherine de Médicis that her noble ancestors Cosimo and Lorenzo de' Medici had placed their library "at the heart of their states, in the city where it was the most accessible to men of learning."[7] The king of France owed it to himself to imitate their example.

The "royal library" was thus a dual reality. On the one hand, in its most solidly instituted form it was intended not for the pleasure of the monarch but for the use of the public. This was how it best served his glory and contributed to his renown. Gabriel Naudé stressed the point in the *Advis pour dresser une bibliothèque* that he had published in 1627:

> [Is there] any more honest and any surer way to acquire great renown among the peoples than by setting up handsome and magnificent Libraries, then dedicating and consecrating them to the use of the public? It is also true that such an enterprise has never deceived or disappointed those who have carried it out well, and that it has always been judged by such consequences, that not only private individuals have done so successfully, to their advantage . . . [and] that even the most ambitious have always desired to make use of it to crown and perfect all their noble actions, as with the keystone that caps the vault and serves as a luster and ornament to all the rest of the building. And I need no other proofs or witnesses to what I say than the great kings of Egypt and Pergamum, Xerxes, Augustus, Lucullus, Charlemagne, Matthias Corvinus, and the great King François I, who all (among the nearly infinite number of the many Monarchs and Potentates who also made use of this ruse and stratagem) enjoyed amassing a large number of Books, sought ways to do so, and had very curious and well-furnished Libraries created.[8]

Like all the great humanist libraries — for example, John Dee's library[9] or the libraries of such French *hommes de robe* (officials, judges) as Henri de Mesmes, to whom Naudé addressed his *Advis*, or Jacques de Thou,[10] both of whom were presidents of the Parlement — the library of the king was not a *solitarium*, that is, a place of retirement from society or a refuge for secret pleasures. Open to men of letters, to scholars, and even to the merely curious (as was the Bibliothèque du Roi after 1692), these collections of manuscripts and printed works could be mobilized to serve knowledge, the rights of the monarch, or state politics and propaganda.

But kings were also readers. That meant that, aside from the "public" library, they had collections of books scattered here and there among their various residences. Fernando Bouza Álvarez has emphasized the contrast between Philip IV's quite personal library in the Torre Alta of his Alcázar Palace in Madrid and the royal library at the Escorial:

> The library of the Torre Alta is without doubt an example of a highly person-
> alized library attentive to the particular and unique characteristics, needs, and
> desires of its proprietor. For the Spanish Habsburgs, the great royal library
> continued to be the Laurentina, and the [library of the] Alcázar fulfilled a less
> representative, more utilitarian and pleasure-oriented function. As Juan Al-
> onso Calderón wrote in 1615, the latter was founded by Philip IV at the
> beginning of his reign precisely "in order to be in it every day," "the king not
> being content with the illustrious Royal [library] of San Lorenzo."[11]

We can see the same duality in France in the contrast between the Bibliothèque du Roi (which Louis XIV visited only once, in 1681) and the
Cabinet du Louvre, later supplanted by the libraries of the Château de
Versailles (created between 1726 and 1729 in the Petits Appartements) and
the Château de Choisy (created in 1742).[12]

*   *   *

The royal collections — whatever their nature — were founded by drawing upon a number of sources. In France these included books confiscated as
a result of victorious military expeditions (for instance, during the Italian
Wars), private libraries of the various members of the royal family (for
example, the library of Catherine de Médicis was included in the royal
collection in 1599, that of Gaston d'Orléans in 1660), new books deposited
by booksellers and printers (a requirement often not respected), books
added by exchanges (such as an exchange in 1668 with the library of the
Collège des Quatre Nations, to which Mazarin had bequeathed his library
and which was reconstituted after the Fronde), and donations (that of the
Dupuy brothers, Jacques and Pierre, in 1652 was the first sizable addition of
printed books to the royal library, which until that point had consisted
largely of manuscripts. Finally, the royal collection also acquired both single
works bought outside France by travelers, diplomats, and correspondents
and entire libraries that had been put up for sale at the deaths of their
owners.

It is another and statistically much less significant source of books for the royal library that interests us here: the book presented to the ruler. The French language uses the same terms — *dédier* and *dédicace* — to designate the consecration of a church and the offering of a book. Furetière's *Dictionnaire universel* (1690) gives these definitions: "*Dédicace*: Consecration of a Church. . . . Is also the preliminary Epistle of a Book addressed to the person to whom one dedicates it in order to beg [that one] to give it protection"; "*Dédier*: Consecrate a Church. . . . Also signifies offering a Book to someone to do him honor and have occasion to speak his praises, and often in the vain expectation of some reward." The ironic, almost bitter tone of Furetière's *espérer vainement* that satirizes penny-pinching patrons and writers in search of a handout must not be allowed to obscure the importance of a practice that long governed the production and the circulation of written works.

In the book itself, the dedication to the prince was an image first. Many frontispieces from the age of the manuscript book show the "author," on his knees before a prince seated on his throne displaying the attributes of his sovereignty, offering a richly bound book containing the work he has written, translated, commented upon, or commissioned. The scene brought a new content to a traditional iconography frequently presented in miniatures, frescoes, sculpted capitals, stained-glass windows, and altar pieces in which a kneeling donor offers a model representing the church or the chapel that he has had built for the greater glory of God. In the picture illustrating the relationship between the sovereign and the writer, the book takes the place of the sacred building, the author replaces the donor, and the king replaces God, whose lieutenant on earth he is.[13]

Cynthia J. Brown has recently suggested that with the coming of the printed book the representation of a dependent author, submissive to the prince who has deigned to receive his work, gave way to a vigorous affirmation of the writer's own identity:

> It seems reasonable to conclude . . . that the advent of print and its development in the late fifteenth and early sixteenth centuries played no small part in the rise of authorial self-consciousness among vernacular writers in Paris. It may ultimately have effected a change in the concept of literature itself.[14]

The example on which Brown bases her thesis is drawn from a work of a Paris "rhetoriqueur," André de La Vigne's *La Ressource de Chrestienté*, an allegoric text written to justify Charles VIII's claims to the kingdom of Naples. In the presentation manuscript to the king (BN MS fr. 1687), the author is both concealed (his name appears only in the final line of the dedicatory verse, and then hidden by a pun) and dependent (the miniature on the frontispiece shows him in the classic posture of the donor kneeling at the feet of the prince).

The printed editions of the same work, which appeared in an anthology titled *Le Vergier d'honneur*, present a quite different image of the author. For one thing, his name figures on the title page and is repeated on the last line of the verse work, where it is given as a personal signature; for another, the dedication scene in the frontispiece has been replaced by a portrait of the author. The woodcut is not an individualized, realistic portrait of the writer but rather a stereotypical "author" shown contemplating his completed work. It is an image that stands on its own, independent of any particular work or any specific author, to designate a generic "author-function," as Foucault called it.[15] A more realistic miniature in a vellum copy of the second edition of the work illustrates the act of composing the work. The poet is seated in a chair similar to the one the king occupies in the usual dedication scenes, and before him appear the allegorical characters who are the protagonists of the work he is in the process of writing — in both senses that the word *écrire* had in fifteenth-century French: physically holding the pen and composing a work. For Cynthia Brown, in the move from the manuscript to the printed book "La Vigne's status as author develops within the same text from a conventionally medieval secondary stance into a growing authoritative presence, and . . . at the same time his patron Charles VIII changes from a dominant, personalized authority to a more absent, ambiguous persona."[16]

Can we generalize on the basis of this example? Perhaps not, if we remember the persistence of such dedication scenes in sixteenth-century printed books. According to Ruth Mortimer's sample of portraits of authors in the sixteenth century, such scenes fall into three types.[17] The first does not, strictly speaking, constitute a presentation of a book, although it does place the author and the king to whom the work is dedicated within a common space. This is what occurs in a woodcut illustrating the *Annales d'Aquitaine* of Jean Bouchet (Poitiers, 1524), where the king (designated in a phylactery as "Franc. Rex") and the author ("Actor") are surrounded by mythological figures ("Mercurus"), allegorical figures ("Fortitudo," "Justitia," "Fides," "Prudentia," "Temperentia"), and historical figures ("Aquitania").[18] The second sort of iconography is in a more traditional vein and shows the act of presentation as the work passes from the author's hand to that of the dedicatee (king, queen, minister, courtier). A third category of illustration shows the author reading his work aloud to the sovereign to whom he is offering it. This occurs, for example, in a woodcut that Antoine Macault used for two translations (one of Diodorus Siculus and the other of Cicero's *Philippics*) that he dedicated to François I.[19] The relationship of patronage and protection shown in dedication scenes thus did not disappear with the first affirmation of the author's identity and the authorial function — an affirmation that predated the invention of print. Such scenes should be seen in connection with the various other ways of portraying the author — pictured alone, pictured surrounded by the real or symbolic attributes of his art, presented as a hero of classical antiquity, or depicted as he looked in real life. The portrait from life that authenticates the work was the choice of the surgeon Ambroise Paré, who, following the example of Vesalius, had himself depicted at various stages in his life in most of the editions of his works that appeared after 1561 (that is to say, in nine of the sixteen editions of his works published during his career as an author between 1545 and 1585).[20]

*   *   *

The contracts drawn up between authors or translators and booksellerprinters are, in their way, another indication of the persistence of dedications to protectors. In the thirty or so contracts written in Paris that Annie Parent-Charon has studied for the period 1535–60, the most frequent arrangement is that the bookseller took responsibility for all expenses and the author received remuneration in the form of a certain number of free copies of this book rather than in cash, the number of copies varying from twentyfive for the translation of Livy's *Décades* (*History of Rome*) by Jean de Amelin, published by Guillaume Cavellat (contract dated 6 August 1558) to one hundred for *L'Epithomé de la vraye astrologie et de la reprovée* of David Finarensis, printed by Etienne Groulleau (contract dated 22 August 1547). Monetary remuneration in addition to the free copies given by the bookseller appears only in two situations: when the author himself had obtained the *privilège* to print the work and had paid the chancery fees, and when the contract was for a translation, particularly one of the Castilian chivalric romances that were in fashion during the 1550s and 1560s.[21]

Even in these cases, however, free copies of the work to be offered to the king and other important personages continued to be the most important item in the contract. We can see this in a clause in the contract drawn up on 19 November 1540 between Nicolas de Herberay and Jean Longis and Vincent Sertenas, Paris booksellers, covering Herberay's translation of the second, third, and fourth books of *Amadis de Gaule*. For his work and for the *privilège* that he had obtained, Nicolas de Herberay received "eighty-four écus d'or soleil" and "twelve unbound [*en blanc en volume de feuille*] copies of each of the aforesaid volumes, as soon as they are printed, without his paying anything." There was more, however: the booksellers promised not to put the book on sale before the translator had time to have a copy of the work that he intended to dedicate to the king bound properly and to arrange for the presentation: "They cannot distribute or sell any of the said three volumes before they have been presented by the said Herberay to the King our Lord, on pain of all expenses, damages, and interests, the which [presentation copies] he promises to offer within six weeks after the said volume is delivered to him, printed and unbound, as specified."[22] Two years later the contract for the translation of the fifth and sixth volumes of *Amadis de Gaule*, signed 2 March 1542 by Nicolas de Herberay and the booksellers Jean Longis, Denis Janot, and Vincent Sertenas, stipulated not only that the booksellers were to pay a sum of 62 écus d'or soleil, but also that they would deliver to the translator "twelve books of the said fifth and sixth books — that is, ten unbound and two bound and gilded — without his having to pay anything for the said books."[23]

The scene depicted in the miniatures and the woodcuts referred to a lasting reality. The king received for his library or libraries a number of works dedicated to him by authors who sought his protection. These authors usually had the books bound before they presented them to the sovereign — a custom that to some extent destroyed the uniformity François I attempted to impose on the volumes in the library at Fontainebleau, all of which were to be bound in the same way with identical decoration on dark brown or black calf bindings, with the royal seal placed at the center of the covers.[24]

Reading aloud the work presented to the king is also an attested practice. La Croix du Maine gives us one example. In 1584 he dedicated to the king (in this case, Henri III) the *Premier volume de la Bibliothèque du Sieur de La Croix du Maine. Qui est un catalogue général de toutes sortes d'Autheurs, qui ont escrit en François depuis cinq cents ans et plus, jusques à ce jour d'huy* (Paris: Abel L'Angelier). Several of the characteristics of this book mark the dependent relationship La Croix du Maine intended to set up between the king and himself. The sovereign's portrait (not the author's) appears in the frontispiece engraving; the dedicatory epistle addressed to the king ends with the words "François de la Crois du Maine duquel l'anagramme est tel Race du Mans, si fidel' a son roi" (François de la Croix du Maine, the anagram of which is "Race of Le Mans, so loyal to its king"). The author even describes what might be yet another dedication scene: "If your Majesty should desire to know what are the other [works] that I have written and composed for the ornament and illustration of your so famous and flourishing Kingdom, I am ready to read (when it may please you to so command me) the Discourse that I had printed five years ago touching on the general catalogue of my works." The "discourse" to which he referred was the *Discours du Sieur de La Croix du Maine contenant sommairement les Noms, Tiltres et Inscriptions de la plus grande partie de ses Oeuvres latines et françaises*, a work listing several hundred books that was published in La Croix du Maine's *Premier volume de la Bibliothèque*.[25] Reading aloud to the king from a work dedicated to him and destined to take its place in his library was an act attesting, even in the age of print, to the persistence of the older meaning of "publication" as a "public" reading of a work before the prince, lord, or institution to which it was dedicated.[26]

The author's dedication of his book to the sovereign was still one of the best ways to win royal goodwill in the eighteenth century. One example takes us to the court of Louis XV. In 1763 Marmontel was lobbying to be elected to the place left vacant in the Académie Française by the death of Marivaux. He was the candidate of the Philosophes, but there were at the time only four of them among the academicians. Worse, one of the king's ministers, the comte de Praslin, was firmly opposed to Marmontel's candidacy. The only way to get around an opposition that powerful was to win the king's backing. In order to do so, Marmontel, the Philosophes' candidate, following the advice of his protectress, the marquise de Pompadour, went back to the most time-honored, traditional gesture of submission on the part of a man of letters and offered the sovereign a richly bound copy of one of his works. As he stated, "the printing of my *Poétique* finally being completed, I begged Madame de Pompadour to get the king to permit a work that our literature lacked to be presented to him. It is, I told her, a favor that will cost nothing either to the king or to the State and that will demonstrate that I am well regarded and well received by the king." The marquise obtained the king's assent without difficulty, and she suggested to Marmontel that he offer his book on the same day to the sovereign, to the royal family, and to the ministers, which was precisely what he determined to do. He set off for Versailles:

> My copies being very magnificently bound (for I spared no expense), I went one Saturday evening to Versailles with my packets. . . . The following day, I

was introduced by the duc de Duras. The king was at his *lever.* Never had I seen
him so handsome. He received my homage with an enchanting look. My joy
would have known no bounds if he had said three words to me, but his eyes
spoke for him.

Furthermore, Marmontel continued:

When I went down to the apartments of Madame de Pompadour, to whom I
had already presented my book, she said, "Go to M. de Choiseul and give him
his copy; he will receive you well. And leave me the copy for M. de Praslin; I
will give it to him myself."

The dedication of the *Poétique* had done its job, as in the end Marmontel
was elected to the Académie.[27] This brief story exemplifies the paradoxical
link, in the eighteenth century, between the new definition of the man of
letters as a fearless practitioner of the philosophic spirit and the respect
for the most traditional forms of patronage that was still necessary for
anyone who hoped to enjoy the favor of the ruler and supreme dispenser of
protections.[28]

*   *   *

Authors and translators were not the only persons who presented
books to princes. The booksellers often did so as well, which meant that
there were times when a dedication put the author of the text and the
producer of the book in competition with each other. Antoine Vérard, a
man who dominated the book-selling scene in Paris between 1485 and
1512, is a case in point. As Mary Beth Winn has shown, Vérard's print
publications presented a certain number of common traits they inherited
directly from the manuscripts that he also produced. For one thing, they
included a dedicatory letter, poem, or foreword that in some instances
figured only in the copy offered to the king; for another, the presentation
copies generally contained a miniature representing the dedication scene.
The important point is that Vérard, who was neither the author of the texts
nor the actual printer of the books but simply their publisher, often cast
himself in the role and took on the posture of the donor. His own portrait
figures in several of the miniatures that show the gift of the book to the
king; in one manuscript his portrait is even captioned *Acteur.* Furthermore,
Vérard signed a large number of dedications to the king (using the formula
"très humble et très obéisant serviteur"). Although in thirteen of the works
he published the dedication to Charles VIII is signed by the author or the

translator of the work, in eleven others (or almost as many) it is Vérard who addresses the sovereign. Antoine Vérard sometimes wrote an original text for his dedications, but he also borrowed preliminary matter written by someone else—and for someone else. Thus in *L'Arbre des batailles* (1493), Vérard presented as his own a dedication written by the author; what is more, the text addressed to Charles VIII had been written for Charles VI. In like fashion, he used the same dedication in two presentation copies of Boethius, *De consolatione* that he published in 1494. The first was addressed to Charles VIII; the second to Henry VII of England, whose name, written in ink, replaced the name of the king of France, which had been scraped away.[29] The bookseller-publishers, considering themselves to be the "authors" of the books whose text they had in fact not written, presented copies of their publications to the prince and to his library as a way of winning his protection. Nor was the practice exclusive to the early days of printing: in the seventeenth century, the bookseller Toussaint Du Bray put a dedicatory letter of his own composition into eight of his publications. Three of them were addressed to a sovereign, two to Louis XII of France and one to Charles I of England.[30]

*   *   *

The dedication and presentation of the book took on a special meaning where scientific works were involved. Galileo provides an excellent example of this.[31] In 1610 Galileo was professor of mathematics at the University of Padua, an institution governed by the Venetian Republic, but his hope was to enter into the patronage system of an absolute ruler, which was the only way to obtain remuneration without having to spend a large part of one's time teaching. The dedication was an essential weapon in the conquest of such a position. In 1610 Galileo published (Venice: Tomasso Baglioni) a work entitled *Sidereus nuncius* in which he described the observations made possible by the *perspicillum* (spyglass) he had devised. The book opens with a dedication to Grand Duke Cosimo II de' Medici, whose protection and support Galileo sought. Galileo offers the grand duke not only his book but also a spyglass to enable the prince to observe the face of the moon, the fixed stars, the Milky Way, nebulous stars, and, in particular, four "planets" (or "stars") that had never been seen before. Even more than the book, what Galileo was dedicating to the Medicis was those "stars"—that is, the four bodies that revolved around Jupiter, as the long subtitle indicated: "quos, nemini in hanc usque diem cognitos, novissime Author depraehendit primus; atque Medicea Sidera nuncupandos decrevit" (which, unknown by anyone until this day, the first author detected recently and decided to name Medicean stars).[32]

By exploiting the dynastic and astrologic mythology of the Medicis that closely associated Cosimo I with Jupiter, Galileo was in fact offering the grand duke what was his, that is to say, "stars" predestined to bear his name. The preface to the work put the notion forcefully: "The Maker of the Stars himself, by clear arguments, admonished me to call these new planets by the illustrious name of Your Highness before all others." Cosimo II was born when Jupiter occupied the "midheaven," and he had inherited the virtues transmitted to the founder of the Medici dynasty by "the star of Jupiter, the most noble of them all."[33] This gift and his skillful dedication brought Galileo what he pined for: five months after the presentation of the book he was named by Cosimo II "Filosofo e Matematico Primario del Granduca di Toscana," a post that bore remuneration as professor of mathematics at the University of Pavia but involved no teaching duties and did not require residence in Pavia. Through the grand duke's ambassadors and diplomats Galileo distributed copies of the *Sidereus nuncius*, accompanied by a copy of the spyglass he had made to accompany the dedication, to princes and prelates all over Europe.[34] The political authority of the dedicatee thus certified and guaranteed the authenticity of the donor's discovery.

As Mario Biagioli has demonstrated, the dedication of the *Sidereus nuncius*, which enriched Cosimo de' Medici's library with a new book, reveals the importance of princely patronage in Europe during the sixteenth and seventeenth centuries.[35] For authors, scholars, and artists, entry into a client relationship, participation in a court, or dependence on a sovereign was often the only way to win an independence unavailable to them through the usual membership in a university or trade guild. It was thanks to the court title he obtained that Galileo could escape the traditional hierarchy of disciplines in the university, which subordinated mathematics to philosophy. Similarly, the painters who hoped to escape guild regulation had no other choice than to become court artists.[36] For those who wrote and published, the offer of a book to the prince was thus an act on which their entire existence might depend. By accepting or refusing the dedication, the sovereign found himself in a position to give or withhold legitimacy to a work (or a discovery). In 1623, when Galileo's new work, *Il Saggiatore*, had been in the process of being printed since March, Prince Cesi and the members of the Accademia dei Lincei (to which Galileo belonged) decided to dedicate and present the work to Pope Urban VIII, elected on 6 August of that year. By the dedication and the distribution of copies of the work to the cardinal-nephew and to other cardinals, Galileo and the academicians of the Lincei hoped to win the approval of the newly elected pope in their quarrel on comets with the Jesuits of the Collegio Romano. They were not disappointed: when Galileo went to Rome several months after the publication of *Il Saggiatore*, he was received six times by the pope; he was also granted authorization (subject to certain demands) to publish the book that was eventually to be his downfall, the *Dialogo . . . sopra i due massimi sistemi del mondo, tolemaico e copernicano*.[37]

The *Sidereus nuncius* bore another lesson as well. By designating himself in the book's title as a "celestial messenger" — a mere courier or mediator giving word of what had always been true but had remained hidden (here, the Medicis' "ownership" of the satellites of Jupiter) — Galileo minimized his own identity as author.[38] This was a tried and true technique in the rhetoric of dedications. One of the many examples one might cite was written by Corneille. The dedication of *Horace*, performed in March 1640 and published in January 1641, is addressed to Cardinal Richelieu. In it Corneille flatters the minister by declaring that the perfection of the latter's ideas and judgments makes them express the rules of theatrical practice:

> You have facilitated our knowledge of [the art of the theater], since we need no other study to attain this than to fix our eyes on Your Eminence when you honor with your presence and your attention the recital of our poems. It is there, reading in your face what pleases and displeases you, that we learn with certainty what is good and what is bad, and derive unfailing rules of what should be followed and what avoided.[39]

The tragedy that Richelieu received in dedication was thus basically the product of his own teaching; by that token, it was his creation just as much as (or more than) it was Corneille's. Whether this rhetoric was an ironic parry or a sincere adhesion to the laws of the genre, it made the king or the great dedicatee the "author" of the work he received; it was one way of inscribing the client-patron relationship within an affirmation of the absolute sovereignty of the prince, who possessed not only what he gave but what he received.

*   *   *

Ordinarily, dedication to the prince involved one particular book that was to enrich his collections, provide him with reading matter, and assure the author his goodwill. In one case that perhaps merits special attention, what was offered to the sovereign was not just one work but a library with the potential to become a royal library. In 1583 François de La Croix du Maine drew up a memoir entitled "Desseins, ou Projects du Sieur de La Croix du Maine, présentez au Trèschrestien Roy de France et de Pologne Henri III du nom" that was published the following year in his *Premier volume de la Bibliothèque*.[40] The text outlines a project for an ideal library, "perfect and accomplished in all points." The library was to comprise one hundred *buffets* (bookcases), "each of them containing one hundred volumes, which will in all number ten thousand, divided into Books, Chapters, Notebooks, and commonplaces, and further reduced to order of A, B, C in order to locate them more easily." The governing principle of the project was the intellectual practice of *loci communes* gathering in notebooks or books citations, examples, references, and observations arranged by topic or theme.

The same intellectual technique dictated the order of the library itself. If the aim, as Fernando Bouza Álvarez has written, was "an exquisite recreation of the universe, whose supreme hierarchy is reflected in that other place in which order has also been created that is the library,"[41] the hundred-bookcase library reached that goal by juxtaposing topics as if they were a hundred headings in a notebook or a commonplace book. In his memoir, La Croix du Maine distributes his materials into seven "orders": "all things sacred, or that depend on such," "arts and sciences," "description of the Universe both in general and in particular," "the human race," "famous men in War," "the works of God," and "miscellanies of various Memoirs." In each of these classifications (whose assigned role in the actual layout of the library is not known), nomenclature is given for the one hundred (actually 108) topics corresponding to the same number of bookcases. This was not a systematic organization of knowledge proceeding by distinctions and divisions, nor was it a hierarchical ordering of the fields of knowledge like, for example, the twenty-one books of Conrad Gesner's *Pandectarum sive Partitionum universalium*, published in Zurich in 1548.[42] Above all, La Croix du Maine's classification furnished categories convenient for an inventory of things sacred and profane.

The second characteristic of the library that La Croix du Maine proposed to the king of France in 1583 regarded its composition. Unlike the royal library as it actually existed, this library was not a collection of original, unique books but an assemblage of ten thousand volumes of manuscript compilations bringing together "all that can be found in writing touching that chosen matter . . . reduced to such a number and such an order that it will be quite difficult to find anything to add to it." La Croix du Maine offered to "furnish Books, Memoirs, or Collections to fill the one hundred bookcases," and he stated that in instances where he had not already gathered and "reduced" the necessary materials it would take no more than eight or fifteen days to put together the contents of any one of his *buffets*. Within each one of these bookcases, the volumes were to be arranged in alphabetical order by subject matter; each volume was to be organized according to the traditional literary divisions ("books" and "chapters"), to material objects ("notebooks"), or to themes (the "commonplaces"). These could be located by the aid of tables or what La Croix du Maine called *mentionnaires* and defined as "like a commonplace book, or collection of Authors who have mentioned particular things." What La Croix du Maine dedicated to the king in 1584 was thus simultaneously a book (his book), a project for a library to serve as an example worth imitating, and the volumes that were to make up that library.

*   *   *

The prince may actually have read some of the many books that were dedicated, presented, and given to him. Froissart reports that on the occasion of his last trip to England in 1395 he offered Richard II a manuscript of his poems.

> He opened it and read it with considerable pleasure, as well he might, for it was beautifully written and illuminated, and bound in crimson velvet with ten silver-gilt studs, and roses embroidered in gold in the center. The King asked the subject of my poems and I replied that they were concerning love. The King was delighted, and read several of the poems, for he read and spoke French fluently. He then handed it to one of his knights . . . and told him to put it in his private quarters. The King was most affable to me about the book.[43]

The dedication scene Froissart describes includes elements often represented by the miniaturists: the author's offering of a manuscript sumptuously decorated and bound; the physical proximity between the prince and the writer (here shown in their exchange of words); the protection accorded by the sovereign to someone who, by the act of the dedication, is admitted into his house or his court. But Froissart's text adds another trait by showing the monarch dipping into the book he has received and indicating his intention to pursue his reading in the private space of his *chambre de retraite*. This testimony confirms what pictorial representations show and forewords "to the reader" had to say about the gains that individual, silent, and purely visual reading had made among the princes and great personages after the mid-fourteenth century.[44]

Having stated that, we should not forget that one of the practices most lastingly and strongly connected with princely libraries was reading aloud to the sovereign.[45] In sixteenth-century France, the person assigned to that task was an office-holder who bore the title of *lecteur ordinaire du roi*. In 1537 Pierre du Chastel, a humanist protégé of Erasmus before he became a protégé of Marguerite de Navarre, succeeded Jacques Colin in that position. Three years later he replaced Guillaume Budé as *maître de la librairie* in the king's library in Fontainebleau.[46] There was thus a direct and immediate connection between the enrichment and the organization of the royal collections and reading aloud at table or during the bedtime ceremony of the *coucher* of the king.

Rabelais alludes to the king's reader in general and to du Chastel in particular in the dedication of the 1552 edition of the *Quart Livre des faits et dits héroïques du bon Pantagruel* that he addressed to Odet de Coligny, cardinal of Châtillon and member of the privy council. While speaking of the accusations of heresy brought against him by "certain cannibals, misanthropes, and agelasts [grouches]," Rabelais declares:

> You were then pleased to tell me that the late King François, of blessed memory, being informed of these slanders, had my books read carefully and distinctly to him by the most learned and loyal anagnost, or reader, in the kingdom. I refer to Pierre du Châtel, Bishop of Tulle, and I say "my" books, because several false and infamous volumes have been evilly credited to me. His Majesty, you told me, found no single passage suspicious. Better still, he abhorred a certain serpent-eater and informer, who based a mortal heresy upon an *n* printed instead of an *m* by the carelessness of the printers.[47]

The last is a reference to chapter 22 of the *Tiers Livre*, where Panurge says of Raminagrobis: "Il a gravement péché. Son *âne* [a typographical error or blasphemous joke for "son *âme*" that appeared in three editions published in 1546 and 1547] s'en va à trente mille panerées de diables" (He is a villainous sinner. . . . He is [lit., His donkey/soul is] shuffling off to thirty thousand basketfuls of devils).[48] Rabelais uses the Greek term *anagnostes*, a word found in Plutarch and in Cicero, to designate the office of Pierre du Chastel, whose readings to the king, as we have seen, concerned not only poetic texts conceived to be spoken aloud but also prose texts such as the "heroic sayings and deeds of the excellent Pantagruel."

We find the same practice at the royal court in England, where the position of "reader to her Majesty" was an envied and hotly disputed office. The correspondence of Lord Harrington gives several indications of this. In 1601 he wrote to Sir Robert Cecil: "I was given to understand by Sir John Stanhope, both that I am bound to you in general for your good opinion, and particularly, that upon the decease of Dr. James, your honor did name me as one you thought fit to be a reader to her majesty." Later, Harrington recalled having given satisfaction to King James I by reading to him one of the cantos of *Orlando Furioso*.[49] Nor were monarchs the only ones who employed readers. Ministers, courtiers, and aristocrats sought out professional readers who could not only read aloud but also offer glosses and commentaries on what had been read or, in the manner of La Croix du Maine, who could serve their patrons by putting together collections, extracts, and commonplace books based on their own reading. The earl of Essex had just such a reader in mind — Lisa Jardine and Anthony Grafton call him a "facilitator" — when he noted, "Hee that shall out of his own Reading gather for the use of another, must (as I think) do it by Epitome, or Abridgment, or under Heads, and common places."[50]

*   *   *

Although it is admittedly marginal in the constitution and the growth of royal libraries, both "public" and more personal, the dedication is a gesture that nonetheless reveals certain of the major interests involved in the collections and the reading matter of the prince and tensions that arose in connection with them. The practice was central to the economy of patronage, which obligated the dedicatee to accord protection, employment, or remuneration in exchange for the book dedicated, offered, and accepted.[51] At a time when the market for works was not yet strongly enough established to permit scholars and men of letters to live by their pens, the favors dispensed by a generous patron were the only way to make one's reputation and find remuneration for one's talents. Nothing shows this better than the bitterness toward the patronage system that underlies Furetière's entry for "Dédicatoire" in his *Dictionnaire*. After a definition (*Dédicatoire*: said only in the phrase, *Epître dédicatoire*, or epistle containing the dedication"), Furetière gives three examples of the use of the term:

Somme dédicatoire or *Traité des Dédicaces* is a satire against the false Maecenases in *Le Roman bourgeois* [an allusion to the title of a parodic fictive work whose table of contents Furetière had given in his own *Roman bourgeois*, published in 1666]. One says that Ariosto and Tasso were very unsuccessful with their dedicatory epistles. Teodoro Gaza received no more than reimbursement for the binding in return for a dedication to Pope Sixtus IV of Aristotle's Book on the nature of the Animals.

The four volumes of the *Somme dédicatoire* that Furetière mentions (a work purportedly found in the library of one Mythophilactes, a writer who died in extreme poverty) contained even stronger criticism as they dissected the laws governing the dedication: "That immoderate praise is of the essence in dedicatory epistles. With the experimental proof that the headiest incense is the one that is found best, contrary to the opinion of the physician-pharmacists" (vol. 4, chap. 2); or, "Whether an author who has given his Maecenas divinity or immortality should be paid twice as much as one who only calls him a demigod, an angel, or a hero" (vol. 4, chap. 7). The text makes sport of denouncing the avarice of patrons as well: "[It is a] most true paradox that the richest lords are not the best patrons. In which is treated the sudden paralysis to which the great are subject and which falls upon them when the question of payment arises" (vol. 2, chap. 11). The work's conclusion is a judgment without appeal that spares no one, not even the king: "Whether the dedication is absolutely necessary to a book. Question decided for the negative, contrary to the opinion of several authors ancient and modern" (vol. 1, chap. 2).[52]

Still, the dedication to the prince is not to be understood simply as the instrument of an unsymmetrical exchange between one person who offers a work and another who accords his patronage in a deferred and generous countermove. It is also a figure by means of which the prince seems himself praised as the primordial inspiration and the first author of the book that is being presented to him, as if the writer or the scholar were offering him a work that was in fact his own. In this extreme figure of sovereignty, the king becomes a poet or a scholar, as was King James I, and his library is not only a treasury for the preservation of threatened wealth, a collection useful to the public, or even a resource for private pleasures. It becomes a mirror that reflects the absolute power of the prince.

3. From Court Festivity to City Spectators

"George Dandin, first time — Tuesday, 10th. . . . The troupe left for Versailles. We played *Le mari confondu*. Returned Thursday, 19th."[1] This is how La Grange, one of Molière's actors, noted the premiere of *George Dandin* at Versailles in July 1668 in the pages of his *Extraits des Recettes et des Affaires de la Comédie depuis Pâques de l'année 1659*.

Under the date of 21 July, the *Gazette* tells us both more and less:

> On the 19th of this month, Their Majesties, and with them Monseigneur the Dauphin, Monsieur, and Madame, and all the Lords and Ladies of the court, having gone to Versailles, were entertained there by the delightful and elaborate festivities that had so long been in preparation and with the magnificence worthy of the Greatest Monarch in the world. The festivities began around seven o'clock in the evening, after a light refreshment deliciously prepared in one of the alleys of the park of that Château, with an excellently put together comedy [*une Comédie des mieux concertée*] put on by the King's Players [*la Troupe du Roi*] in a superb theater set up in a vast open-air hall in the shrubbery. This comedy, which was mixed into the entr'actes of another sort of comedy with music and ballets, left nothing still to be wished for at this first Entertainment, at which a second light refreshment of fruits and sweets heaped into a pyramid was served from the two sides of the Theater and presented to Their Majesties by the lords who were placed on it. This was accompanied by quantities of playing fountains, and was found utterly gallant by the nearly three thousand Persons present, among whom were the Papal Nuncio, the Ambassadors presently here, and the Cardinals Vendôme and Retz.[2]

The *Gazette*, which mentions neither the title of the play nor its author, and which gets the date wrong (the royal festivities were held on 18 July, not 19), nonetheless tells us a good deal about the context of the premiere of *George Dandin*.

It was a moment of monarchic triumph. In February of that year, the king's armies had conquered Franche-Comté from the Spanish in a swift campaign. Besançon surrendered to Condé and Salins to the Duke of Luxembourg on 7 February; Dole capitulated before the king on 14 February, Gray on the 17th. As Louis XIV noted in his *Memoirs* (or as his secretary wrote from his own notes and from the journal dictated by the king), the entry into Gray put an end, "in fifteen days of winter, [to] a conquest that, being undertaken with fewer precautions, might have stopped me in more than one campaign." On 24 March, the dauphin had been baptized at Saint-Germain-en-Laye; on 2 May, the Peace of Aix-la-Chapelle had been signed. By the terms of the treaty, France ceded Franche-Comté back to Spain (after dismantling its fortresses), but kept a dozen Flemish towns and cities that it had conquered the previous year, among them, Lille and Douai. As Louis XIV explained, "Franche-Comté, which I handed back, could be reduced to such a state that I could be its master at any time, and my new conquests, firmly established, would open a more certain entry into the rest of the Low Countries."[3] The king, still a young man, played to perfection all the ideal roles of the monarch: victor in war, guarantor of dynastic succession, and triumphant peacemaker.

The next task was to exhibit the king's glory so that all could read, hear, and see it. Writers of verse rallied to the cause. At Rouen, six poets — Pierre Corneille among them — had published a collection of poems in Latin and French (printed by Laurent Maurry) entitled *Au Roy sur sa conqueste de la Franche-Comté*. At Versailles, in late April, Molière and his troupe played, for the pleasure of the sovereigns, *Le Médecin malgré lui*, *Le Mariage forcé*, *L'École des femmes*, *Cléopâtre* (a tragedy written by one of the actors in the troupe, La Thorillère), and *Amphytrion* (played for the first time on 13 January in the palace of the Tuileries). The April performance of *Amphytrion* was preceded by the reading of a sonnet written by Molière celebrating the conquest of Franche-Comté, which concluded:

> Mais nos chansons, Grand Roi, ne sont pas si tôt prêtes,
> Et tu mets moins de temps à faire tes conquêtes
> Qu'il ne faut pour les bien louer.

> (But our songs, Great King, are not ready so soon, / and you take less time to make your conquests / than [we] need to praise them properly)[4]

The poems glorified the king's victories; the Fête de Versailles was to celebrate the peace. It took from May to July to prepare for it, for its magnificence was to demonstrate to all — grandees of the realm and foreign ambassadors — that the king was master of pleasures as he was of armies, that he could offer magnificent amusements as generously as he granted peace, that he was supreme in both expenditure and power. In this entertainment calculated to overwhelm the senses, the theater had its place. As was normally the case, a play was demanded from the "King's Players" — *la troupe du roi* — instituted in August 1665 with a pension of 7,000 livres (Molière received 1,000 livres a year, listed under the heading of "pensions and gratifications for men of letters"). The subject of the comedy would have to fit without incongruity into the program of the festivities, which were to take place in the park, and the play must also make people laugh. In order to respect the pastoral theme of the celebrations, Molière chose a village tale: that of *George Dandin*.

The comedy must have pleased Louis XIV, since he ordered its reprise in November 1668 to celebrate St. Hubert's Day. La Grange noted: "On Friday 2 November, the troupe went to Saint-Germain-en-Laye, where the company played *Le Mari confondu*, otherwise [known as] *George Dandin*, three times, and *L'Avare* once. The return was on the 7th of the same month. Received from the king 3,000 l[ivres]."[5] The *Gazette* mentioned that the St. Hubert's Day festivities on 3 November were "accompanied by the Ballet and the Comedy that had served for the charming treat at Versailles, along with a marvelous symphony. The next day, and the two days after, Their said Majesties continued this agreeable entertainment, which was again followed by the Comedy, with Ballet entries, and by a most gallant ball."[6]

Two days after the troupe's return to Paris, *George Dandin* was performed in the hall of the Palais Royal, which had been given over to Molière in October 1661 (and which he shared with the Comédiens Italiens after that company returned to Paris in January 1662). The play was given without the *entrées de ballet*, alone or coupled with another comedy, on ten occasions between 9 November and 9 December 1668.

George Dandin was performed in two forms in 1668, for two quite different audiences. At the court, the comedy was part of a larger cycle of celebrations of the monarchy; intermixed with music and ballets, it was only one festive moment in a series of varied pleasures. In the city, the play entered into another universe — the world of the urban theater, which (in Paris, at least) had its own permanent halls, its annual calendar, and its established repertory. The same text was thus given under totally different conditions of representation, each mobilizing its own unique and utterly different expectations and references. Hence the first step toward understanding *George Dandin* requires a reconstitution of what its two sets of spectators in 1668 might have made of it as they constructed a meaning for the text. In contrast to a critical tradition indifferent to the ways in which texts are put into print or performed, the dual inscription of *George Dandin* into the court festivities and in the city theater reminds us that no work has any meaning outside of the varied forms that offer it for decipherment. Just as a text radically changes meaning, even when its letter remains unchanged, by differences in its typographical presentation, its format, the layout of its pages, its illustrations, and the distribution of its parts,[7] the meanings of Molière's comedy varied quite evidently according to the devices of representation that bent the play to their own forms. This is already a reason for reconsidering *George Dandin*, but it is not the only reason.

George Dandin has had a career full of paradoxes. Twentieth-century critics have not shown much interest in it: excluded from the corpus of Molière's greatest works, it has inspired very few studies, and those few have pursued the usual avenues, identifying possible sources or exploring its comic mechanisms.[8] There is one notable exception: Lionel Gossman devotes a chapter to *George Dandin* in which he proposes an overall view of the play. For Gossman, the comedy belongs to the "*Bourgeois Gentilhomme* type," because its protagonist seeks the recognition of people whose superiority he accepts, rather than to the "*Misanthrope* type," in which a protagonist who depends on no one seeks an absolute superiority that transcends all social conditions.[9]

But if the critics have neglected the play, theater people have shown a lively interest in it. Since World War II three productions have made it obligatory to take another look at the play: one by Roger Planchon at the Théâtre de la Cité de Villeurbanne in 1958; another by Jean-Paul Roussillon at the Comédie-Française in 1970; and a third, in 1987, again by Planchon at the TNP (Théâtre National Populaire).[10] Each production was unlike the others in its intellectual intentions and its dramatic solutions to the play's problems. In 1958, Planchon emphasized the class relations among the various characters (Dandin, the peasant who had become rich; the Sotenvilles, penniless gentlefolk; and Clitandre, the arrogant courtier), but he also focused on the domination exerted by masters of all sorts over peasants whose lot was endless labor and who, walled in by silence, lived a closed-in life. Roussillon was more interested in showing the characters' tragic fate — Dandin, bewildered and ridiculed, furious and powerless, but also Angélique, delivered over to Dandin by her parents, a victim in revolt. The social reading of the first production brought a realist profusion, peopling the stage with peasants who might have come from a painting by Le Nain; the scenery for the second production was austere and frigid, a setting for a painful tragedy. Beyond their stylistic differences, however, these two productions (which inspired many imitators) both stated that, despite appearances, *George Dandin* is not a comedy designed simply to make people laugh, but rather a cruel play that strips bare society's ills. When he returned to the play in 1987, Planchon attenuated its tragic aspects, but still treated it as a serious play. He saw the play as a "photograph, or an X-ray, of a couple in crisis" and as "the first example of a play that spoke of the heart's indecision."[11]

This was a far cry from the *comédie bien concertée* that Molière was commanded to write for the amusement of the courtiers and that was given in the park at Versailles one July evening in 1668. And yet, is that so sure? Molière made people laugh, but was laughter all he had in mind? Or, rather (to avoid vain discussions about the author's "intentions," which cannot be known, especially in this case, and which, in any event, could not possibly include the entire meaning of the work), might not the text of *George Dandin* be a discourse on society that could have no other place in the seventeenth century? That is the hypothesis of this study: it postulates a compatibility between an "action" (Molière's term for stage business, what acting adds to a text) that aims at setting off laughter, on one hand, and, on the other, a subject that implies representation of the mechanisms by which social relations are constructed. In the seventeenth century, comedy in the theater could treat subjects that were treated later in very different forms of discourse (sociological discourse, for example). The real subject of *George Dandin* might be: what is the truth about a social order that is perceived in contradictory ways by social agents who mistake its true hierarchies? Or, from the opposite point of view: how does multiple blindness, translated into decisions and acts, shape the dominations and dependencies that are, for those who experience them, the reality of social relations, whereas another way of perceiving society shows them to be illusory or laughable?

Thus the first idea that underlies this study is that literary texts offer a representation of contradictory principles of construction of the social world and of the categorizations by means of which individuals, in a given situation, act to classify others and, by doing so, classify themselves. The same sort of thing occurs in the novel, in tragedy, and in comedy, but the three genres are not the same. The dictionaries of the late seventeenth century—Richelet's dictionary, published in 1679; Furetière's, published in 1690; and the *Dictionnaire de l'Académie*, of 1694—explain how they differ. These definitions make a first distinction between the novel, which is related to the fable, and tragedy and comedy, which belong to the order of representation. Whether the definition of the novel is more favorable, as with Richelet, or more negative, as with Furetière, it evokes the ideas of invention, lack of verisimilitude, and imagination: "The novel is today a fiction that includes some amorous adventure, written in prose with wit and according to the rules of the epic Poem for the pleasure and the instruction of the reader" (Richelet); "Now [the term] is restricted to fabulous books that contain stories about love and chivalry invented to entertain and occupy the idle" (Furetière); "*Roman*: work in prose containing fabulous adventures of love or war" (Académie). The novel unfolds its plot and presents its characters within a literary convention that had no need to respect verisimilitude in its action or its emotions.

To the contrary, if tragedy and comedy are "representations" it is because they give a true image and a reliable account of the actions of men and women. The difference between the two forms lies in the object they represent. Tragedy supposes "illustrious" protagonists and famous acts situated outside the bounds of the common condition. Richelet: "Tragedy . . . is a sort of poem that represents a serious action, complete and just in its grandeur, and that, by the true imitation of some illustrious misfortune that excites terror, pity, or both together, instructs the spectators agreeably." Furetière: "Dramatic poem that represents on the stage some signal action by illustrious persons that often has an unhappy ending." Académie: "Dramatic poem, theatrical piece, that represents a grand and serious action between illustrious persons, and that usually ends with the death of someone among its principal characters." In Molière's day, ancient history, mythology, and the Bible offered privileged sources for raw materials for heightened actions and illustrious persons sufficiently well-known to guarantee that their representation would be grasped and appreciated, but sufficiently remote that their portrayal did not have to conform to the audience's self-image.

Molière built his contrast between tragedy and comedy on precisely the lesser duty to verisimilitude that historical distance gave tragedy. In *La Critique de l'École des Femmes*, speaking through Dorante, he states:

> When you portray heroes, you can do just what you please. These are fanciful portraits; no one looks for lifelike resemblances in them. You merely have to follow the suggestions of your roving imagination, which often abandons the true in order to pursue the marvelous. But when you are painting men, you must paint them from nature. Everyone insists that the likenesses resemble reality; and you haven't accomplished anything, unless you make your audience recognize the men of our own time.[12]

On the one hand is freedom of imagination, liberation from the constraints of the "true," and the possibility of inventing sentiments and situations not analogous to those of common experience; on the other, the need to respect a common knowledge about the social world (or, at least, knowledge shared by potential spectators) that serves to evaluate whether a specific act or plot complication resembles life, whether it partakes of the order of the "true" and not of the "marvelous." By implication, Molière shifts the dividing line the dictionaries placed between the novel (like a fable) and both tragedy and comedy (representing human actions) to place the novel and tragedy together, since neither is held to the demands of "imitation of the real," and contrast them with comedy, which paints from nature.

For the dictionary definitions, the object of this painting is something close to the person looking at it: it is "a common action" (Richelet), "persons of middling condition" (Furetière), "an action in human life that takes place between private persons" (Académie). Nonetheless, the situations portrayed must not be taken as real (or even possible); that proximity supposes that the ways of perceiving and hierarchizing the social world that the author gives to his fictional characters will seem comprehensible, decipherable, and likely for the spectators who watch them act. The "truth" of comedy does not lie in equating theatrical plots with situations that actually occur in the real world, but rather in a compatibility between the classifications in action produced by the characters and the acts of classification by which what happens on stage makes sense within the different modes of reception of the various publics who attend performances of the play.

This hypothesis forms the base for a "historical reading" of plays — here, of *George Dandin*. But "historical reading" has led to so many misunderstandings that we need to state what is meant by it here.

For me, it involves weaving together three strands of analysis. The first strand involves a consideration of gaps: the gap between the text of the comedy and the other texts — literary and other — on which the comedy was constructed, and the gap between situations in the theater and situations in the social world that served as their matrix. The second strand is the forms in which the text was given: at a festive evening for the court or on the stage of the Palais-Royal; published separately, in its first editions, or as part of Molière's complete works; printed with text alone or accompanied by illustrations. The third strand is how the comedy was received — receptions attested in contemporary accounts and others we can only guess. This will require investigating, on the basis of a certain number of sets of documents and within a limited time, how the text of the comedy led its spectators or its readers to mobilize a social knowledge fed by current events and based on ways of perceiving and judging the mechanisms that create hierarchy and social mobility. Thus it will require moving from the contents of the text and from discourses and practices on which the text is based toward the thoughts that those contents were capable of eliciting. But it will also require noting, in the contrasting forms of representation, anything that operated outside the text to lend it meaning. The first of these forms was the court festivity.

*   *   *

> First, one saw on the stage a magnificent refreshment of Portuguese oranges and all sorts of fruit in thirty-six baskets loaded to the bottom and [heaped] in pyramids, which were served to all the court by the Maréchal de Bellefond, and by a number of lords, while the Sieur de Launay, the *intendant* charged with the lesser amusements and affairs of the chamber, gave out, to all sides, printed booklets containing the subject of the comedy and the ballet.[13]

These anonymous *imprimés* in the form of a program were printed by Ballard, "sole Printer to the King for Music"; the piece was titled "Le Grand divertissement royal de Versailles: Sujet de la comédie qui doit se faire à la grande fête de Versailles."[14] The spectators at Versailles on 18 July 1668 found in this booklet (after praise of the king, a "great king in everything") the plot of the comedy, summarized act by act, and the text of the sung portions of the entertainment. Conceived as a program of the premiere and distributed before the performance, the booklet also served to publicize the spectacle afterwards, as Robinet's *Lettre en vers à Madame* of 21 July of that year attests:

> Et, pour plaisir plus tôt que tard
> Allez voir chez le sieur Ballard,
> Qui de tout cela vend le livre,
> Que presque pour rien il délivre,
> Si je vous mens ni peu ni prou;
> Et se vous ne saviez pas où
> C'est à l'enseigne du Parnasse.

(And, for pleasure sooner rather than later, / go see at Ballard's place — / who sells the book about it all / for practically nothing — /

whether I am lying to you at all. / And if you don't know where, / it's at the sign of Parnassus.)[15]

For its readers, the comedy — which bears no title here — was thus reduced to a summary of its plot, whereas the entire text of the musical scenes was given. It was only in 1669, after the first performances in Paris, that the text of *George Dandin ou le Mary Confondu* was published, without the text of the sung portions. Jean Ribou published the first Paris edition, and it was immediately pirated, in particular by the Elzeviers in Amsterdam.[16]

Le Grand divertissement royal begins with praise of the monarch in the obligatory parallel between conquest and festivity. He displayed the same glory, he acted with the same éclat, he elicited the same astonishment in both: "There is something of the hero in all that he does; and even in pleasurable matters, he shines with a grandeur that passes anything hitherto seen." The festivities at Versailles had several aims: to be a fitting ornament to the peace the king had conceded in response to his subjects' pleading; to present in its full brilliance the king's immense power to dispense favors; to represent, in its arrangements, his other and more warlike exploits. All the sovereign's acts were prodigies that bent time to his law and nature to his will:

> You have seen on our frontiers the provinces conquered in one winter week and powerful cities overcome along the way; here we see emerging, in less than no time, in the middle of the gardens, superb palaces and magnificent theaters, enriched on all sides with gold and with great statues, enlivened by greenery and refreshed by a hundred fountains.

Ballard's booklet does not detail these *merveilles*, because "one of our fine minds is charged with giving an account of them" (Félibien, who was to describe the décor for the Fête de Versailles after the event).

The program kept to the comedy. It gave its author: "It is Molière who wrote it. As I am one of his good friends, I find it fitting not to say anything good or bad about it, and you will judge it when you see it." This statement, which allows us to attribute the entire spectacle — the sung parts as well as the prose acts — to Molière, also suggests that he was the author of the booklet published by Ballard, or that he at least had taken a close look at the text. This means that *Le Grand divertissement royal* is important as an indication of what Molière had to say about his play (or had someone else say) even before the premiere. He describes it in two ways. First, it is an *impromptu de comédie*, written under the pressure of a royal command. To note this was to appeal to the spectators' indulgence, but it also suggests that the way the actors put life into the text is more important than the text itself, and that the play ought to be seen rather than read: "I will say only that it would be desirable for [the play] if everyone viewed it with the eyes needed for all comic impromptus, and if the honor of having obeyed the King swiftly might serve, in the minds of the hearers, as part of the merit of these sorts of works." In this respect *George Dandin* resembled other comedies written for the king and his pleasures. One of these was *L'Amour médecin*, written in 1665, the printed text of which is preceded by a foreword, "To the Reader," that could stand for all theatrical works written under the same conditions:

> This is only a bare Sketch, a sort of an Extempore, of which the King was pleased to make a Diversion. . . . It was Proposed, Written, Learn'd, and Acted in Five Days. . . . 'Tis generally known that Comedies are only writ to be Acted; and I wou'd have no Body read this but such as have Eyes to discover the Acting in the Reading of it.[17]

As a sketch or an impromptu, *George Dandin* was inscribed within a genre with few surprises and whose intentions and conventions fell under clear rules.

Nonetheless, the comedy was innovative, even in its form. Indeed, its "subject is mixed with a sort of comedy in music and ballets," a genre that, as Molière (or his mouthpiece) notes, is not to the taste of the nation and might "startle the minds of the French." Hence the reference to the "sentiments of the connoisseurs who have seen the rehearsal" and who much appreciated the inventiveness of Lully's music and choreography. Hence, also, the publication of the text of the sung portions so that spectators unfamiliar with that type of declamation could follow along. For Molière there was no explicit hierarchical gradation between the two forms, the comic impromptu and the comedy in music and dance. The spectacle was a mixture of both. Still, when it came to summarizing what the audience was about to see, he speaks of *George Dandin* alone: "The subject is a Peasant who has married the daughter of a gentleman and who, throughout the comedy, is punished for his ambition." There is a measurable distance between this definition of the spectacle, which gives autonomous life to the play, and the report published in the *Gazette*, which does not mention the name of the play or summarize its plot, but states that the comedy "was mixed into the entr'actes of another sort of comedy with music and ballets," thus granting the more inclusive role to the nobler form.

The theatrical spectacle presented on 18 July 1668 could thus be defined in two ways. Was it a comic play embellished by sung and danced interludes? Or was it a *comédie en musique et de ballets* whose entr'actes were filled by a comic impromptu in prose? The two descriptions imply a different perception: did the court in the park at Versailles attend a comic performance about a peasant who married above his station or a spectacle of songs and dances whose "plot" was, in the last analysis, unimportant? And if the first version is the right one, was this story simply a reprise of a traditional comic situation and a comic type, as the socially neutral title that La Grange noted, *Le Mari Confondu*, suggested, or is it better understood as the story, adapted to the stage, of a specific social rise and fall — that of the peasant "punished for his ambition" — as the program booklet indicated? These differences in the definition of the genre and the subject matter of *George Dandin* (that is, the *George Dandin* of July 1668) may appear small, but they show that from the outset there were contradictory perceptions of the play. It seems clear, in any event, that the categories that Molière used to describe his play (or to have someone else describe it) were not the same as those of the chronicler who wrote an account of the royal festivities for the *Gazette*.

But *Le Grand divertissement royal* also had the aim of informing the spectator, accustoming him or her to the mixture of comic theater and comedy in music, and "explaining the order of all that." It makes it clear that the unities of time and place would be respected: "The entire affair takes place during a great fête champêtre." Here is how this account organized and commented upon the various sequences of the two intermingled plots:

1. *Overture*: dance of four shepherds "disguised as footmen" that interrupts the reveries of the peasant husband and forces him to withdraw.

2. *Chansonette* of Climène and Cloris, "two shepherdesses and friends."

3. *Scene with music* in which Cloris rejects the love of Philène, and Climène the love of Tircis. The two shepherds, in despair and "following the custom of the lovers of antiquity, who fell into despair for little reason," decide to kill themselves:

> Puisqu'il nous faut languir en de tels déplaisirs,
> Mettons fin en mourant à nos tristes soupirs.

(Since we must languish in such agony, / let us put an end to our sad sighs by dying.)

4. First act of the comedy: "The married Peasant receives humiliations because of his marriage, and toward the end of the act, deeply afflicted, he is interrupted by a Shepherdess, who comes in to recount the despair of the two Shepherds. He leaves her in anger, leaving the stage to Cloris."

5. *Complaint in music*: Cloris deplores the death of her lover:

Quoi donc, mon cher amant, je t'ai donné la mort,
Est-ce le prix, hélas! de m'avoir tant aimée?

(What? My dear lover, have I killed you? / Is that the price, alas! of having loved me so?)

6. Second act of the comedy: "It is a succession of misfortunes for the Peasant husband, and the same Shepherdess does not fail to come once more to interrupt him in his unhappiness. She describes how Tircis and Philène are not dead, and she shows him six Boatmen who have saved them. He refuses to stay to see them."

7. Dance of the Boatmen, "delighted by the reward they have received."

8. Third act of the comedy, "which is the height of the sufferings of the married Peasant. Finally, one of his friends advises him to drown his anguish in wine, and leaves with him to rejoin his flock when he sees approaching the whole throng of Shepherd lovers who, like the Shepherds of antiquity, sing and dance in celebration of the power of Love."

9. Celebration of Love by Cloris, Climène, Tircis, Philène, and the chorus of love-smitten Shepherds; then celebration of Bacchus by the chorus of Bacchus. "Combats of dancers against dancers, and singers against singers." Alternating songs from Cloris and a follower of Bacchus; of the chorus of Love and the chorus of Bacchus. Final reconciliation of the two parties after the song of a Shepherd:

L'Amour a des douceurs, Bacchus a des appas,
Ce sont deux déités qui sont fort bien ensemble
Ne les séparons pas.

(Love has its sweetnesses; Bacchus has charms. / They are two gods
who go well together: / let us not separate them.)

The joined choruses sing the finale together:

Mêlons donc leur douceurs aimables,
Mêlons nos voix dans ces lieux agréables,
Et faisons répéter aux Echos d'alentour
Qu'il n'est rien de plus doux que Bacchus et l'Amour.

(So let us mix their lovable sweetnesses; / let us blend our voices in
this lovely place, / and make the Echoes all around repeat / that
nothing is sweeter than Bacchus and Love.)

The booklet concludes: "All the dancers mingle together, following the
example of the others, and with this celebration of all the Shepherds and
Shepherdesses the comedy ends, after which one will pass on to other
marvels still to be related." This last was a way to announce another text, the
one written by Félibien, historian of the buildings (and the pleasures) of
the king.

Is there any "order in all that"? Molière manages to establish connec-
tions and consonances between the plots of the pastoral and the comedy,
beginning with the fiction of a country celebration that makes a story about
love-struck shepherds compatible with a tale about a peasant unhappy in his
marriage. There are also correspondences in sentiments: Dandin's mortifications echo the despair of the two shepherds; his recital of his woes
recalls Cloris's. The parallel is broken at the end, however, in an opposition
between the mismatched husband's irremediable suffering and the pleasures promised to more harmonious lovers. Finally, when Dandin chooses
to forget the torments of his unfortunate marriage in wine, he prefigures, in
his way, the combat of Bacchus and Love that gives the spectacle its musical
finale. There, too, the fate of the unhappily married peasant diverges from

that of the love-struck shepherds: Dandin can only replace love with wine, whereas the shepherds know how to combine Bacchus and Love.

Contrary to what has often been stated, there are specific elements that tie together the two plots.[18] Moreover, the disparate forms of the prose comedy and the comedy in music of July 1668 repeat a procedure that Molière had already used in *Amphytrion*, created six months earlier. In both works he represents the behavior of valets and masters, inferiors and superiors, rustics and great personages in comparable situations. In this light, George Dandin, the humiliated husband, is the comic double of the love-struck shepherds. Like them, he is afflicted; like them, he is driven to despair by a woman. But he has no verse and no music to express his unhappiness, and neither his language nor his soul have the delicacy of the heroes of the pastoral. His grief is without remedy — outside inebriation — and he can never know the felicity reserved for chosen lovers. Like Sosie and Mercury before them, like Sganarelle and Dom Juan later, Dandin and the shepherds express the unbridgeable gap separating social conditions and qualities. In the 1668 *divertissement*, the difference in forms (pastoral and comedy, song and recitation, verse and prose) translates into the terms of theatrical spectacle the radical difference between the shepherds, who love in the manner of the court, and a peasant whom no one would dream of loving. The impatience that Dandin shows repeatedly, when he "leaves in anger" when a shepherdess comes to tell him of the despair of Tircis and Philène, and "refuses to stay to see" the boatmen who have saved the two lovers, clearly shows the incompatibility of the two worlds of the pastoral and the comedy and of the Arcadian heroes and ordinary men. Hence the mixture of forms that Molière and Lully proposed for the festivities of July 1668 has a meaning over and above the obligations due the king's command and the requirements of the entertainment. There was indeed "order in all that," an order that pointed a moral of distinction and of the absolute separation between the aristocracy, of the soul and of birth, and common humanity.[19]

Still, the very laconic summaries given of each act of *George Dandin* in *Le Grand divertissement royal* tell us more — or something else — than this interpretation. The vocabulary it uses is never taken from the grotesque or even the comic: Molière speaks of the *mortifications* (humiliations) of Dandin in Act I and of his *chagrin* (affliction) and his *colère* (anger); for Act II, he speak of his *déplaisirs* (misfortunes) and his *douleur* (unhappiness); for Act III, "the height of the *douleurs* (sufferings) of the married Peasant," he speaks of his *inquiétudes* (anguish). The vocabulary used to describe Dandin's sentiments is that of tragedy; the words, used in their strong sense, speak of the torments of the soul and the mind of illustrious heroes. *Chagrin* and *douleur* are terms frequent in Racine's works; Corneille often uses *déplaisirs*.[20] *Mortifications* and *inquiétudes*, on the other hand, belong to the vocabulary of sacred rhetoric and spiritual literature, where they speak of the misery of the human condition. Finally, *colère* is taken from the language of the passions of the soul: in Descartes's *Traité des passions*, the word describes one particular passion, and both Corneille and Racine use it in this sense. There is nothing trivial about Dandin's afflictions and emotions in the booklet published by Ballard, and the terms used are drawn from lexical registers usually foreign to comedy. Hence this comedy's unfortunate hero cannot be taken for the stock figure of the ridiculous husband of farce.

As we have seen, Molière summarizes (or has someone summarize) the subject of his comedy in purely social terms that inscribe it within contemporary reality. It is the story of a peasant who has married the daughter of a gentleman. Moreover, Molière describes his hero's sentiments with a vocabulary taken from the noble genres. This means that later interpretations of the play in a sociological or a tragic vein are not arbitrary inventions: they are present even in the text of the program distributed to the king and to the court on the evening of the play's first performance. On the other hand, the comedy was given to amuse that august company, and Molière — playing the part of Dandin — had to elicit laughter. Because it was set within a pastoral of a conventional sort, the impromptu had to participate in the imaginary and abstract world of *bergeries* — tales of shepherds and shepherdesses. This is enough to baffle anyone, and it has proved enough to produce a broad variety of interpretations, some seduced by theatrical forms, which see *George Dandin* as the sum of a pastoral and a farce, others more sensitive to the ambiguities inherent in the text itself, which muddles distinctions between the genres and is presented as a literary work on the social world. Accounts of the fête given on 18 July may help give us an idea of how the court viewed the comedy.

*   *   *

The first and most official of those accounts is the one written by Félibien and hinted at in *Le Grand divertissement royal*. The purpose of Félibien's work was to relate, to the king's subjects and to the world at large, the magnificence of the royal fête. It was published anonymously, a few days after the fête, by Pierre Le Petit, "Printer and Bookseller ordinary to the King, rue Saint Jacques at the Golden Cross."[21] There are two known

printings in 1668, which differ only in their title page.²² The account was
reprinted in 1679 under the imprint "De l'Imprimerie Royale par Sébas-
tien Mabre-Cramoisy, Directeur de ladite Imprimerie." The latter edition,
where this account joined other descriptions of festivities to form a print
memoir of royal celebrations, was printed in the quintessentially noble
format of the folio volume. The text was signed, and the account was
illustrated by five engravings by Lepautre, as had been promised in 1668:
"The public will be given the figures of the principal decorations." In order
to attest to the sovereign's grandeur to the entire world, the fête needed to
be put into book form. Still, the image to be gotten of it by reading the text
or viewing the illustrations was powerless to represent all that it had been,
and Félibien concludes his account: "One must not think that the idea that
one forms of it by means of what I have written about it in any way
approaches the truth."

Félibien's account situates the place and the role of the comedy within
the overall arrangements of the evening much better than *Le Grand divertissement royal*. He begins with the reason for the Fête de Versailles, which
was not immediate celebration of the peace treaty but a reward for the
court:

> The king, having granted peace at the urging of his allies and the wishes of all
> Europe, and [having] given the signs of a moderation and a goodness without
> peer, even in the thick of his conquests, had no other thought than to apply
> himself to the affairs of his kingdom when, in order, so to speak, to make up for
> what the court had lost during Carnival during his absence, he resolved to have
> a fête in the gardens of Versailles.

We learn here that the festive calendar of the court reflected that of the
commonality, and the royal *divertissements* were set to coincide as much as
possible with the canonical times of folk culture. Court civility was also a
carnival culture that recognized (in different forms) the same calendar
cycles and the same symbolic dates as townspeople and villagers. This was
the case at the beginning of 1668: on 5 January, the eve of the Fête des Rois
(Ephiphany), the court had attended a performance of *Le médecin malgré
lui* at the Tuileries; on the 6th, Epiphany, a comedy, a concert, and a supper
were given in the king's apartments; on 18 January, again at the Tuileries, *Le
Carnaval*, a "royal masquerade" by Benserade was performed (the king
himself participating), and the ballet was performed a second time at Saint-
Germain the next day. After that, the campaign of Franche-Comté interrupted the normal cycle of carnival festivities. The fête on 18 July was

thus something like an afterthought to make up a festivity deficit for the year. Comedy, an obligatory element of carnival at court, was a necessary presence.

The king's intention was to have the comedy fit into a variety of entertainments: it was to be preceded by a refreshment and followed by a supper, a ballet, and a fireworks display. The king chose the spots for these in the park at Versailles, seeking places "where the disposition of the place could, by its natural beauty, contribute more greatly to their decoration." He picked water as the chief element of the evening, "because one of the most beautiful ornaments of this house is the quantity of waters that art has brought here, in spite of nature, which had refused them to it." He also outlined the program, which was to be a multiple celebration of Nature, obliterating the customary frontiers between nature and artifice. The entire fête was to be a rustic amusement in which natural beauty would be subjected to the rules of art and decorative artifice would appear to be the work of Nature itself.

The program of the fête was a pathway leading the king and the court from one amusement to another. At each stop, they would find a place, a pleasure, and an architecture, all ephemeral.

George Dandin, which in itself was intertwined with a comedy in music and ballets, was thus set into a bigger framework of a court fête with a complex program, multiple episodes, and a bewildering array of marvels. Félibien, aware that words were inadequate to describe such a wealth of beauty, attempted an inventory, and his description is like a detailed and maniacal bookkeeper's account of candles and candle-holders, basins and playing fountains, buffets and services, ornaments and figures. He used numbers to try to give an idea of the grandeur of the fête and to give "an image" of it that was necessarily imperfect, but that might suggest both the infinite munificence of the king and his power to command even the elements. Under his rule, the murmur of the waters harmonized with the sound of the musical instruments, and fire mixed with water.

As a festive merging of differences, a celebration of expenditure,[23] and a feast of surprises for the senses, the 1668 *divertissement* was typical of the first phase at Versailles. The ballroom, decorated with arrangements of rocks and seashells and cascading waters, resembled the Grotto of Thétis, where a water organ, polychrome stones, and glittering mirrors enchanted both the ear and the eye. All around the château of Louis XIII, the gardens that Le Nôtre had created and filled with baths and fountains, basins and statues, offered an ideal setting for a celebration of Nature, but a Nature who took orders from the sovereign.[24] The symbolic scheme of the decorations was charged with proclaiming just that. Symbols developed a coherent program from one setting to another. Nature was represented as mythology with Pan, Flora, and Pomona; satyrs and fauns; tritons and nymphs, and as the cosmos with allusions to time (the four seasons, the twelve months "with the signs of the zodiac," the four parts of the day) and space (the four parts of the world, the four major rivers of the world). The sun god Apollo reigned over this throng of gods and goddesses, elements, and seasons. Apollo was figured twice at the fête: a first time on top of a rock placed at the center of the supper hall, where he appeared with lyre in hand and surrounded by the Muses, and again symbolically in a "sun with lyres and other instruments connected with Apollo" placed at the summit of the façade of the illuminated château.

The 1668 fête was a court festive function of a sort often considered the hallmark of baroque civilization. It reiterated many of the characteristics of courtly entertainments all over Europe between the fifteenth and the eighteenth centuries[25]: the demonstration of power through expenditure, the pleasures of the ephemeral, appearances taken for reality and reality become illusion, and distinctions made highly visible by the distribution of ranks and roles (in particular, in the seating arrangements of the supper tables). Like court etiquette, the fête was a way to make clear the absolute difference between the court, which enjoyed it, and the rest of society, which was excluded from it; it was also intended to give visible form to the gaps among those who shared the privilege of being near the sovereign. Above all, it was meant to celebrate the glory of the great king who was its supreme patron.

The Fête de Versailles of 1668 added a few touches of its own to the usual outline for the court festivity. It was an exaltation of Nature with its decorations of leafy branches and flowers, its cascading waters, its profusion of things to eat, and its shepherds out of a pastoral. By installing this rustic illusion in a real garden, by organizing an endless abundance, by offering, for one evening, the delights of an antique and ideal nature, the fête both expressed and circumscribed the nostalgic reveries of a nobility whose duties as courtiers had torn them away from the liberty (real or supposed) of a previous life on their lands. Like the chivalric romance or the pastoral, the fête, in its various forms, could be understood as a utopian reversal of the constraints imposed by court life; it was a momentary denial, by means of fiction, of the new obligations of an urbanized aristocracy brought to the court.[26] During the 1660s, however, the increasing ritualization of life at the court at Versailles marked a further step in the subjection of the nobility to an existence that was no longer chivalric or rustic. To emphasize this subjection (while seeming to deny it momentarily), the king twice proposed festivities that focused on the noble existence of times past: in May 1664, with *Les Plaisirs de l'Île Enchantée*, in which the king and the courtiers played the roles of the warrior knights in *Orlando Furioso*, and in July 1668, with the Fête de Versailles, a celebration of nature and waters in which the court enjoyed a rustic world of beauty and abundance.[27] By doing so, Louis XIV captured and turned to his own profit the nobility's nostalgia for a former life of warlike or pastoral values, once declared in contrast to court life and lived away from the court, which paradoxically became the basic substance of an evening's entertainment, shaped by the king's command and arranged according to rules governing their new life as courtiers.

There was another significance in the 1668 fête, however: it was one of the mechanisms for solidifying the parallel between the young king and Apollo, the god of the sun. This myth was built up in clearly marked stages. In 1663, Le Brun decorated the Gallery of Apollo at the Louvre; in 1666, Girardon and Regnaudin received the commission for a sculptural group for Versailles, "Apollo Attended by the Nymphs," to be placed in the Grotto of Thétis; about the same time, Mignard and Loyr painted the decorative panels (one of which was "Apollo Resting with Thetis") for the Hall of Apollo and its antechamber in the Louvre.[28] The 1668 fête, by suggesting, at every stage and in every setting, a connection between the god and the king, both masters of harmony, prosperity, and beauty, brought the solar qualification of the victorious king and peace-bringer to its peak. The sovereign must have been pleased, since afterwards the decision was made to build a new château on the garden side of the old one, and the park was reorganized along an Apollonian axis joining the Grotto of Thetis, the Basin of Latona at the center of the Rondeau, and, at the foot of the gardens, the Basin of Apollo, which contained a large statue of the god in a chariot drawn by four horses.

George Dandin, set within its pastoral, was only one of the moments of this fête of multiple meanings. Félibien went back to the program published by Ballard for his presentation of the intertwined plays. Like the Ballard text, Félibien gave the text of the sung portions in their entirety, and he summarized the three acts of *George Dandin* in much the same terms. Still, there are several notable differences between the two texts. First, Félibien describes the décor in which the pastoral and the comedy took place.[29] When the canvas that concealed the stage was raised, the spectators' "eyes were totally fooled, and they thought they were in fact seeing a garden of an extraordinary beauty." Vigarini's *trompe l'oeil* made use of the same figures and the same architectural elements for the stage set as for the decorations of the supper hall and the ballroom.

In this way, the stage set established a continuity between the rest of the evening's entertainments and the comedy. In its smaller space, it replicated the larger spaces inhabited by the court. It used the same materials (marble, bronze), identical decorative elements (flowers, trees, water), and similar architectural figures (a terrace, a garden walk, a canal); it set an illusory garden within a true garden, and its stage scenery was constructed within the other construction of the theatrical space in which the comedy was played. This interplay of correspondences, analogies, and nested motifs in the 1668 fête bears traces of an older formula for organizing the pleasures of the court and a theatrical plot within one space and one scenic décor. Something similar had occurred in May 1664, when the three days of *Les Plaisirs de l'Ile Enchantée* abolished all difference between the fiction played by the actors (*La Princesse d'Elide*) and the fiction that the king and the grandees themselves played, on an outline borrowed from Ariosto, combining various amusements — jousting for the ring, refreshments, the comedy, the ballet, and the fireworks — "with connection and order." In 1668, the king and the courtiers did not dance the pastoral, but the similarity of the settings within which the false shepherds and the true gentlemen, the ladies of the court and the peasants of the comedy, all moved created a space for illusions in which the ordinary divisions between reality and artifice were blurred. *George Dandin* was performed in a setting that had no relation to the social or the spatial indications in the text. It took place in an ideal space that (like the Arcadia of the musical *bergerie*) must have weakened the effect of reality of its plot.

Nevertheless, when he describes the subject of *George Dandin*, Félibien, who amplifies the summary in *Le Grand divertissement royal*, maintains the same, completely social, register: "The subject is that a rich Peasant, being married to the daughter of a country gentleman, receives nothing but scorn from his wife and from his father-in-law and his mother-in-law, who have taken him as their son-in-law only because of his great wealth." This description offers in two ways from the program distributed to the spectators. First, the social characterization of the characters is more specific here: the peasant has become a *riche paysan*; the gentleman is a *gentilhomme de campagne*. Second, the reason for Dandin's unhappiness has been shifted. He is no longer "punished for his ambition" and the agent of his own sorrows, but the victim of others — of his wife and of parents-in-law who scorn him. The subject is thus dual (the peasant's misplaced ambition and the financial calculations of the country squires) and its meaning is transformed (from a well-earned punishment to suffering inflicted by others). In Félibien's quintessentially "courtly" reading, the Sotenvilles risk becoming the principal agents of the plot: it is their scorn that causes Dandin's torments.

For Félibien, the subject of what was performed was precisely that. To be sure, Félibien states that there was a formal unity between the pastoral and *George Dandin*: "Although it seems as though these are two comedies being played at the same time, one in prose and the other in verse, they are none the less so well united into the same subject that they make one single play and represent one single action." But Félibien adds that the prose comedy was itself a play — *une pièce* — whose written style had nothing in common with pastoral style:

> All of this play is treated in the same manner as is customary in le sieur de Molière's other plays — that is, he represents in it, with such natural colors, the personality of the characters he introduces that nothing could be more true to life [*ressemblant*] than what he has done to show the anguish [*peine*] and the vexations [*chagrins*] often experienced by those who marry above their station. And when he paints the ill-temper and the manners of certain country nobles, he presents no traits that fail to express perfectly their true image.

Although Félibien sees the comedy as linked, in a number of ways, to festive illusion, he also presents it as a work that springs from a different order — the order of truth, of a true-to-life portrait, of an accurate image. The truth he evokes is not that of the psychological portrait, but that of social behavior patterns — the *manières de faire* of one social group or another. This postulates a relationship between the theatrical work and the social world that is inscribed in the register of the "representation" and that supposes a radical difference (situations and characters are not real) but enough of a concordance that an "other" reality can be perceived in the specific fictional forms presented. This explains how the two dimensions of *George Dandin* could have been compatible in the eyes of a seventeenth-century audience: as fiction, the comedy could belong fully to the world of theatrical illusion, be connected with a pastoral involving shepherds and shepherdesses, and take place in a "marvelous" setting; as representation, it referred back to something other than its forms and spoke truth about social situations.

There are two other reports of the festivities of July 1668 that invite comparison to Félibien's account. The first was written by Abbé de Montigny at the request of the queen and published in 1669 in a composite collection printed in The Hague. Montigny was particularly charmed by the way in which the settings that had been erected in the park reflected a simple nature unspoiled by civilization: the *théâtre de verdure* was "an edifice of rustic appearance that, rising almost to the level of the tops of the trees and having no other exterior decoration than what had been stripped from forests and gardens, effaced the pomp of palaces and gave brilliance to simple country things." He also admired the realization of things that seemed impossible: the hall in which the supper was offered was "a sort of enchanted palace of a structure as rare and singular as anything the authors of romances have ever imagined"; the *cabinet de verdure* in which the refreshment was taken "owed more to the enchantment of the Fairies than to human industry. Indeed, no one was to be seen when the company entered; all that could be glimpsed through the palisade was hands that appeared with shining trays to offer something to drink to anyone who wished it. Everyone paused a while to marvel at this device."[30] This was a reminder of a noble nostalgia for the pleasures of a free, agrarian past, but also of the formidable powers of a magician king, successor to the magician god, Apollo.

Abbé de Montigny summarized the comedy, played before "an incredible crowd of spectators," thus: "Molière's troupe played one of his sort, new and comic, agreeably mixed in with songs and ballet interludes in which Bacchus and Love, after vying a while to get the better of one another, finally reached an agreement to rejoice together." Montigny reverses Félibien's presentation: here the subject of the pastoral is summarized and the theme of the comedy is not even mentioned. At best, Montigny mentions that the play was "comic" — something that neither *Le Grand divertissement royal* nor Félibien's report specified in their summaries of its theme. In those texts it was taken for granted that the play elicited laughter, not because it was inherently comic but because of its "action," that is, the acting and the stage "business" that defined its genre. Where, for Montigny, the play he had seen could be summarized by defining its form (to the point of not mentioning its subject), for Molière and for Félibien the essence of the work was not in its implicit respect of a genre — being "comic" — but in the particular situation that was represented.

Like Abbé de Montigny's report, Robinet's *Lettre de vers à Madame*, a verse *gazette* that appeared since 1665 (picking up a formula that had proved successful during the Fronde), qualifies the play as "comic" without giving its subject:

En ce beau Rendez-vous des jeux
Un Téâtre auguste et pompeux
D'une manière singulière
S'y voyait dressé pour Molière
Le Mome cher et glorieux
Du bas Olympe de nos Dieux.
Lui-même donc, avec sa Troupe,
Laquelle avait les Ris en croupe,
Fit là le Début des Ebats
De notre Cour pleine d'Appas,
Par un Sujet archi-comique
Auquel rirait le plus stoïque,
Vraiment, malgré-bongré des Dents,
Tant sont plaisants les Incidents

(In that handsome meeting-place for pleasures, / a theater august, magnificent, / and singular / was erected for Molière, / the dear and glorious Momus / of the nether Olympus of our gods. / He in person, with his troupe / and all their laughter in the saddle, / started off the festivities / of our charming court / with a superlatively comic subject / that even the most hardened stoic would truly laugh at, / willy-nilly, / so amusing were its plot twists.)[31]

Also like Montigny, Robinet gave a summary only of the "comedy in music and ballets" that belonged to a more noble genre than Molière's "little comedy," thus clearly distinguishing between the pleasure brought by dancing and singing and the laughter elicited by the *incidents plaisants* of the comic plot. He thus saw *George Dandin* as a traditional farce, *archi-comique* because it offered (in the last act in particular) a series of surefire stage routines (repeated misunderstandings and reversals) and because its characters (or some of them) conformed to the tried-and-true types of comic theater. The role that Robinet picked out for special comment was not that of Dandin or even the Sotenvilles, but that of the servant, Lubin, "played by La Thorillière, who was recovering from an illness" and who "was undoubtedly the funniest."

The first series of texts — a program booklet, an article in the *Gazette*, an "official" account, another one written at the request of the queen, and a *gazette en vers* — shows two distinct ways of perceiving *George Dandin* (that is, the *George Dandin* performed in July 1668, mixed in with another plot and inserted into a multifaceted festive evening). For the *Gazette*, Abbé de Montigny, and Robinet, what had been performed (and seen) was a "comic," even "superlatively comic" play that made people laugh thanks to its "action," but whose subject was so unimportant that it did not merit mention. The play's worth was as part of a series of airs and ballets leading up to the combat between Bacchus and Love. *Le Grand divertissement royal* and Félibien's account define the play in quite different terms: first, by its subject, which they describe in social terms; second, by its style of presentation, which aimed at a truthful, natural, and true-to-life representation of situations and persons who belonged to the social world, not — or not only — to theatrical tradition. On the one side, the comedy is defined by its "amusing plot twists" and its comic outline; on the other, it is a play that was, above all, an "image" (and a critique) of contemporary reality.

Which of these two plays did the court see in 1668? We cannot tell for sure from eyewitness accounts. The Dutch physician Christiaan Huygens attended the festivities, but he was so impressed by other aspects of the evening that he seems not to have been too interested in the play. He wrote:

> The fireworks were what I found most beautiful, never having seen such a quantity of rockets filling the air at one time. The comedy by Molière, whose subject was the cuckolding of a peasant who had married a lady, was hasty and not much, but the hall and the stage were very handsome, as were the two other octagon-shaped halls made of scaffolding and decorated with leaves, festoons of flowers, paintings, and fountains, one for the dinner, the other for the ball.

Huygens concluded, more prosaically than the gazettes and memoirs:

> I had left home at five in the morning and did not get back until the next day at seven, having suffered great heat and great cold during the same night, not slept at all, and eaten in haste, with the result that my fatigue was not small, but my consolation was that everyone else had suffered in the same fashion.[32]

For Huygens, the social relationship in *George Dandin* could be brought down to a classic situation of the comic theater: the ridicule of the cuckolded husband. His vocabulary is not that of the passions or of compassion (as with Félibien), but rather the vocabulary of farce and the bawdy tale: Dandin is a cuckold, and the play is "not much." Huygens thus differs from the reader implied by *Le Grand divertissement royal* or by Félibien. Huygens saw nothing of the meaning of a comedy that aimed at making people laugh (as goes without saying), but that inscribed that laughter into a *morale*, as Bénichou would say, or into a "representation of reality," as Auerbach would say.[33]

As for the king, he laughed. Perhaps at Versailles; certainly at Saint-Germain. Robinet reports about the performances of *George Dandin* given on Saint Hubert's Day, in early November 1668:

Au reste l'on dit que Molière,
Paraissant dans cette Carrière
Avec ses charmants Acteurs,
Ravit ses Royaux Spectateurs
Et, sans épargne, les fit rire,
Jusques à notre grave Sire,
Dans son Paysan mal marié
Qu'à Versailles il avait joué.

(Furthermore, people say that Molière, / appearing in that place / with his charming actors, delighted his royal spectators/ and made them laugh heartily, / including our serious Lord, / at his ill-married Peasant / whom he had played at Versailles.)[34]

*   *   *

We need to see what that laughter was all about, and, in order to do that, we need to understand the story and let ourselves be taken in by the effect of reality that the comedy intends to produce. We need to act as if Dandin had a history behind him, a memory, and an existence. And, at the same time, we need to realize that he is merely a theatrical figure, a "representation" fashioned by the imagination and by writing; that he is arbitrary yet true-to-life, true-to-life yet arbitrary. Thus we need to read what he says not as what a "true" peasant who had married a "real" daughter of a country gentleman would have said. Theatrical fiction does not aim at reproducing a "real" situation; it hopes to enable its audience to seize, behind the illusion that it both postulates and denies, the contradictory procedures by which social reality is constructed.

This is what George Dandin himself has to say:

Ah! qu'une femme demoiselle est une étrange affaire, et que mon mariage est une leçon bien parlante à tous les paysans qui veulent s'élever au-dessus de leur condition, et s'allier, comme j'ai fait, à la maison d'un gentilhomme! La noblesse de soi est bonne, c'est une chose considérable assurément; mais elle est accompagnée de tant de mauvaises circonstances, qu'il est très bon de ne s'y point frotter. Je suis devenu là-dessus savant à mes dépens, et connais le style des nobles lorsqu'ils nous font, nous autres, entrer dans leur famille. L'alliance qu'ils font est petite avec nos personnes: c'est notre bien seul qu'ils épousent, et j'aurais bien mieux fait, tout riche que je suis, de m'allier en bonne et franche paysannerie que de prendre une femme qui se tient au-dessus de moi, s'offense de porter mon nom, et pense qu'avec tout mon bien je n'ai pas assez acheté la qualité de son mari. George Dandin, George Dandin, vous avez fait une sottise la plus grande du monde. Ma maison m'est effroyable maintenant, et je n'y rentre point sans y trouver quelque chagrin.

(Ah! It's a proper business and no mistake to wed a member of the nobility; my marriage is a clear warning to all those of farming stock who want to rise above themselves and marry into a noble family as I have done. Not that there's anything wrong with the nobility in itself; it's a fine institution; but it's got so many unfortunate aspects that it's a good thing not to rub up against it. I've become all too knowledgeable on this subject to my own cost, and know how the nobility treat the likes of us when they receive us into the families. They hardly marry themselves to us as persons at all; it's only our money they marry, and I would've done much better, rich as I am, to find a match in good and decent yeoman stock than to take a wife who believes herself to be my social superior, who takes umbrage at having to bear my name, and thinks that with all my money I still haven't paid out enough to deserve the rank of husband. George Dandin, my old fellow, it's the stupidest thing in the world that you've done! Your own house has lost its charm for you, and whenever you go home, you find some cause or other for complaint.)[35]

Thus, from his very first monologue and from the first scene in the first act of the play, George Dandin tells us both why he is so discouraged and — for those who know how to listen — what is the true subject of the "comic" or "superlatively comic" play. His marriage is a "clear warning" and an opportunity to become "all too knowledgeable" at his own cost. And what is this new and painfully acquired wisdom that has cost him so dear? It is an insight that society does not function as he had supposed. His marriage with a *demoiselle* from a noble family was based on a simple perception of social relations in which any modification of the visible acquisitions of a social being is a necessary and sufficient condition — necessary, but sufficient — for everyone to accept his rise on the social scale. Dandin could not claim to be noble by his marriage, but by entering into an aristocratic family, and by bearing a seigneurial title, he had hoped to be recognized as (thus truly to be) the equal of those with whom he had sought and obtained an alliance. A certain number of "objective" and "verifiable" transformations in his social person—he *is* the son-in-law of a gentleman; he *is* a lord and landowner—should, by that fact, change the way in which others categorize him and esteem him. By modifying, by his own will, the attributes of his social identity, he attempts to impose a new and obligatory representation of himself as ennobled, if not noble.

That matrimonial strategy was founded on a perception of the social world that is both mechanistic and labile. Mechanistic, because it supposes the existence of necessary laws and automatic equivalences that regulate the passage from one social condition to another. The operation that Dandin attempts to carry off was to convert an economic capital—which explains all the insistent reminders: "tout riche que je suis"; "avec tout mon bien" ("rich as I am"; "with all my money")—into a social capital measured by the recognition that other people give him. This sort of operation is based on a belief in objective mechanisms that by themselves and without fail are capable of creating changes of identity, mechanisms capable of transforming a rich peasant's social identity and others' perception of him and of making him the equal of the gentleman into whose family he has married. This vision, in which there is no gap between what someone thinks he is and what others think him to be, postulates that social mobility is possible, that it is legitimate to act to change one's social status, and that certain acts (marrying into the nobility, acquiring seigneurial lands) are an authorization to rise above one's condition and be considered as belonging to another, more honorable, more highly esteemed condition.

But experience teaches that this conception of the social world is a complete illusion. Marriage has taught Dandin that there is no point to thinking he can define his own social status, because the standards of classification and judgment by which he is identified are wholly in the eyes of others—in particular, in the eyes of a dominant "other" from whom he hopes to gain recognition of social, if not juridical, equality. Thinking that it is possible to manipulate one's social status by changing its attributes is a trap—or a folly—because status depends above all on the decrees of those who are in a position to say, by their words or by their behavior, what status is.

As the monologue progresses, Dandin shows that he has understood this. At the start, his "I" is strong ("comme j'ai fait"; "as I have done"), which recalls that it is illusory to imagine a society in which the intentions and acts of a social agent give him full control of his own social being. With the third sentence, everything has changed, and Dandin switches from being the "subject" of his own story to being the "object." It is as if the "ils"

("they") that expresses the will of the nobles took away all his self-posses-
sion. Like others of his kind ("nous autres"), he is forced to have a social
identity imposed on him that he cannot control, that is not the one he
thought he had won, and that is by no means in tune with his hopes.

Social proximity, even when it is formalized by marriage, even when it
is signified by a certain tenor of life, is not enough to bring "real" equality,
which is the recognition of social equality on a practical level and in ordinary, day-to-day life. Dandin's vocabulary mentions gaps ("au-dessus";
"above") and inequality ("pas assez"; "not enough") to express dashed
hopes and illusions. Dandin's relations with Angélique are the most obvious (and the most cruel) sign of this, because their conjugal life is by no
means experienced as a recognized equality, and the difference between
their social status reverses the "natural" hierarchy that should exist between
husband and wife ("une femme qui se tient au-dessus de moi"; "a wife who
believes herself to be my social superior"). In spite of marriage, financial
capital has not been transformed into social capital, as shown in the brutal expression of the failure of his attempt to communicate: "[elle] pense
qu'avec tout mon bien je n'ai pas assez acheté la qualité de son mari" ([she]
thinks that with all my money I still haven't paid out enough to deserve the
rank of husband). But the idea that conjugal or social status can be bought,
and, by that token, depends on the buyer, is laughable. Social classification
is not an objective transaction between equal partners. It is a "nomina-
tion"—one is named to it—that presupposes an unbridgeable distance
between the person who holds the power to name and the person who is
named. The gap between the representation constructed and imposed on
the individual and the representation he has of himself is irradicable.

Differences in social status are thus absolute and insurmountable.
Dandin draws the lesson that mobility is impossible by advocating (too late
for himself, however) a philosophy of social stability that leaves the "estates" radically separated: "J'aurais bien mieux fait, tout riche que je suis, de
m'allier en bonne et franche paysannerie" (I would've done much better,
rich as I am, to find a match in good and decent yeoman stock). The "ill-
married" peasant reflects here the idea, common at the time, that a well-
regulated society supposed permanent "conditions" (thus, supposed marriage alliances between social equals, and sons equal in status to their
fathers). Dreams of equality with the nobility are chimerical: it is better
"not to rub up against it." Exchange is unequal between superiors and
inferiors and cannot be otherwise, because the superiors have no intention
of conferring any of their "honorableness" to their alliances by marriage,

but only to turn some of their wealth to their own profit: "L'alliance qu'ils font est petite avec nos personnes: c'est notre bien seul qu'ils épousent" (They hardly marry themselves to us as persons at all: it's only our money that they marry).

Social relations and social classifications do not obey the principles that Dandin supposed, which leads to a disenchantment that he immediately translates into psychological terms: "Ma maison m'est effroyable maintenant, et je n'y rentre point sans y trouver quelque chagrin" (My own house has lost its charm for me, and whenever I go home I find some cause or other for complaint). The vocabulary that Molière uses is strong, violent, and borrowed from tragedy: *effroyable* means that which "gives fear, terror, horror" (Furetière); *chagrin*, which Félibien also uses, indicates extreme displeasure, "anxiety, pain, melancholy" (Furetière again). But this disillusionment is translated in another dramatic way by the doubling of the character, who speaks to himself: "George Dandin, George Dandin, vous avez fait une sottise la plus grande du monde" (George Dandin, my old fellow, it's the stupidest thing in the world that you've done). All commentators have noted Dandin's habit of addressing himself as a major trait of his character.

At first sight, talking to oneself might seem a comic technique inherited from farce. *La Jalousie du Barbouillé* also opens with a monologue in which the main character speaks to himself: "Ah! pauvre Barbouillé, que tu es misérable! Il faut pourtant la punir. Si je la tuais? . . . L'invention ne vaut rien, car tu serais pendu. Si tu la faisais mettre en prison? . . . La carogne en sortirait avec son passepartout. Que diable faire donc?" (Ah, poor Barbouillé, how miserable you are! Still, she has to be punished. What if you killed her? That would do no good, for you would be hanged. What if you had her put in jail? The good-for-nothing would get out with her passkey. What the devil should you do, then?) Here we have none of the social connotations of *George Dandin* because Barbouillé imputes his unhappiness to his wife's behavior alone; still, the text plays on the same comic effect of a man who talks to himself out loud. Molière used this technique on several occasions, from Arnolphe's monologue in *L'École des femmes* (III.5) ("Sot, n'as-tu pas de honte?"; "Have you no shame, fool?") to Harpagon's monologue in *L'Avare* (IV.7), where the doubling of the character is physical, since Harpagon grabs hold of his own arm ("Il se prend lui-même le bras"), a "gag" that may be a device for stifling the audience's pity for a character who is deceived, desperate, and miserable.[36]

In another interpretation, this doubling, which appears in the three monologues of the first act of *George Dandin*, should be understood as the expression of a duality in the character himself. It is an expression of contrary aspirations: the Dandin who speaks wants to make known his intolerable situation and obtain justice; the Dandin to whom he speaks idolizes the Sotenvilles and has thought, for a moment, that he could share a little of their glory. The first Dandin, the one who rushes to "désabuser le père et la mère" ("complain to her father and mother") is willing to humiliate himself in order to humiliate those who have betrayed his hopes; the second Dandin recalls his vain hopes — not vain because they recognized the superiority of gentlefolk, which is something that Dandin never questions, but because he thought it possible that his in-laws could accept him as an equal.[37] The duality of Dandin can also be seen as an opposition between a "wisdom" acquired too late and an irremediable "folly" that haunts his memory. In this interpretation, the doubling of the character is an indication of the passage of time; the silent trace of an irreparable error; and the primordial reason, always recalled, for humiliations endured and for the expiation he must perform.[38] This would explain Dandin's difficulty in communicating with others, his deep-seated solipsism, and his "linguistic alienation."[39]

But there is another possible way to read this dialogue of a character with himself: as the dramatic expression of a statement about how society works. The Dandin who speaks in the present tense is the one who knows how the determination of social identity really operates in daily contacts, which is by the regard and the conduct of those who hold power. The Dandin to whom he speaks is the one who had thought the impossible might be possible, who placed absurd hopes in an illusory perception of the mechanisms that regulate esteem, hence social reality. Once he recognizes his mistake, the character constructs another life in his imagination — the life he might have had if the Dandin of "then" had known what he knows "now": "J'aurais bien mieux fait, tout riche que je suis, de m'allier en bonne et franche paysannerie" (I would've done much better, rich as I am, to find a match in good and decent yeoman stock). That marriage, now impossible but brought up again when Lubin confirms Angélique's interest in Clitandre ("si c'était une paysanne"; "if she were only a peasant"), is for Dandin the desirable but unreal inversion of a real but dreadful situation. Thus the two contradictory perceptions of social classification are tied together: the one, illusory, that sees that classification as depending on the will of the individual, and the other, the one Dandin has experienced, that sees it as a mechanism of domination. The two strategies of marriage alliance that correspond to those two views are also merged: the one that erroneously thought change of social condition possible and the one that recognizes the need for social condition to remain the same. The *mortifications*, the *déplaisirs*, and the *douleurs* of the married peasant mentioned in the program distributed to the assembled courtiers do not arise uniquely from the twists of a plot that subjects him to humiliation on three separate occasions; they also express the inexorable trajectory of a destiny built on a false idea of the social world and its laws.

*   *   *

Any understanding of what the court audience first, then the Paris audience, may have understood of this discourse on the rules for the construction of social hierarchies or social equality presupposes that we relate that discourse to the perceptions of the character speaking. The play is not a treatise on sociology, and every speech in it is like a pencil-stroke in the "good likeness" of the theatrical character's portrait. Some critics do their best (in vain) to identify a character in each play who speaks for Molière or speeches that express his own opinions. It is wiser to keep in mind Uranie's warning to Climène in *La Critique de l'École des femmes*:

> Climène: Je vous avoue que je suis dans une colère épouvantable, de voir que cet auteur impertinent nous appelle des *animaux*.
> Uranie: Ne voyez-vous pas que c'est un ridicule qu'il fait parler?

> (Climène: I admit that it makes me frightfully angry that this impertinent author should call us "animals."
> Uranie: Don't you see that he puts that in the mouth of a ridiculous character?)[40]

In our case, it is a peasant speaking, proclaiming how rich he is and that he has married a gentleman's daughter. But what other hints are given to the audience to help it "classify" the character who is speaking?

Unfortunately, no contract for the set design seems to have been offered (as in December 1664 for the "ouvrages de peinture" for *Dom Juan*) that might give us an idea of the scenery for the Paris performances of *George Dandin*, but the probate inventory drawn up between 13 and 21 March 1673 gives us some idea of the costume in which Molière played the "mismatched peasant." On 14 March the notary inventoried the theatrical costumes; among them was "a box in which are the clothes for the performance of George Dandin, consisting in britches and coat of musk-colored taffeta, with a collar of the same, all decorated with lace and silver buttons, the belt the same, the small vest of crimson satin, the other vest of different colors of brocade and silver lace, the ruff, and shoes."[41] This costume, which has nothing of the peasant about it, would immediately have been recognized as an exaggerated, forced, and old-fashioned imitation of aristocratic dress. With its abundant lace (something not found in Molière's costumes for Orgon or Alceste), many colors (also true of the costumes for Monsieur Jourdain and Pourceaugnac), and old-fashioned *fraise* (ruff) (the only other costume that had one was Sganarelle's in *Le Médecin malgré lui*), Dandin's clothes also signify the character's vain attempt to become something he cannot be. By its ridiculous excess and archaism, the costume exhibits the unbreachable distance separating Dandin from those he would like to resemble. His most visible act of imitation shows — immediately — how totally impossible his new identity is. Brisart, who drew the first series of engravings for an edition of Molière's works, the edition of Denis Thierry, Claude Barbin, and Pierre Trabouillet based on a manuscript provided to La Grange by Armande Béjart, illustrates the overly ostentatious wealth of Dandin's costume (minus the ruff, however). Pictured in the next-to-last scene of the play, the scene of his final humiliation, a young looking Dandin with curled hair, on his knees, wears lace at his cuffs and his neck, an over-vest with a bizarrely ornamented pocket, and shoes with oversized laces. Although it may be less obvious in the engraving than it probably was on the stage, Dandin's costume clearly suggests his hapless and exaggerated identification with "the noble style." Social imitation is always labeled as such; betrayed by its excessive awkwardness, it is in an appearance of proximity that difference is maintained.

Dandin is first a costume, then, a laughable costume because of its inappropriate attempt to plagiarize noble clothing. Dandin is also a name, and a name that bore two connotations. The first echoed the root sense of the verb *dandiner*, which, for the *Dictionnaire de l'Académie Française* (1694) meant "to shake one's head and one's body as simpletons [*niais*] usually do, and those who have no countenance." Furetière's dictionary (1690) defined *dandin* as "Great fool [*sot*] who has no firm countenance; who makes rude movements with his feet and hands" ("qui a des mouvements de pieds et de mains déshonnêtes"). Richelet's dictionary, which was the one closest in time to Molière himself, defines *dandin* as "a sort of fool [*sot*] and simpleton [*niais*] who goes about looking here and there. A sort of booby [*benêt*] and dullard [*lourdaud*] who appears listless and witless." Richelet illustrates *dandiner* with an extract from Saint-Amant: "Il dandine du cul comme un sonneur de cloches" (in colloquial English, "He swings his butt like a bell-ringer"). The example recalls one of the proposed etymologies of the word *dandin*, which, in the fourteenth century, meant a small bell. His name, which even has a comic sound to it, thus indicates that the peasant is a ridiculous fool who vacillates between a nobility he admires and a commoner's status he cannot shake off; it hints that he will be tossed back and forth in plot twists in which he will be duped and will forever oscillate between an exaggerated imitation of gentlefolk's ways and the rusticity natural to the peasant.

Furetière adds a second connotation: "Rabelais wrote a History of Perrin Dandin and Thénot Dandin, from which a moral is drawn that is much used in good society for all who wish to resolve law-suits." "Dandin" is thus a literary name, used by Rabelais in Chapter 41 of the *Tiers Livre*, used again by Racine in *Les Plaideurs* (first performed in October or early November 1668), and used ten years later by La Fontaine in his *Fables* (Book 9, number 9). In all three cases the name is associated with the law. Rabelais's Perrin Dandin is an "honorable soul, a good plowman" who was much called on to settle "all disputes, lawsuits, and controversies" for miles around, "although . . . judge he was not." His son Thénot "likewise tried to mediate and reconcile litigants," but he was less successful than his father, because he attempted to settle disagreements "at the beginning when they are still green and raw" rather than toward their end, when they are "quite ripe and digested" and the contending parties were exhausted, short on funds, and ready to compromise.[42] Racine's Perrin Dandin is a real judge, the scion of a long line of Dandins "who have all worn the toga" and a man so eager to judge that he becomes deranged. By using this name, associated in literature with the function of judge, Molière may well have wanted to play on the tradition (undoubtedly familiar to at least some of his audience) by turning it upside-down: his Dandin is not a judge but judged, three times judged guilty by Monsieur de Sotenville, a "natural" judge.[43] George Dandin is like a Dandin in reverse; not a dispenser of justice but always the victim of the justice that he himself has demanded in his (erroneous) certainty of his rights. This comic name, in its fashion, denies the possible reality of the character and his situation just as much as the pastoral that framed the play at Versailles did in its way. Dandin is indeed a "seigneur," but an imaginary one who bears the ridiculous title of "Monsieur de la Dandinière." How better could Molière have indicated that if his play contained a representation of the social world, that representation by no means avoided the comic conventions that dissociate characters from their supposed real models.

One of the strongest of those conventions was the one that shaped the representation of the peasant and made him immediately identifiable for audiences of both city and court. Molière's use of the convention to draw the character of Dandin was subtle. When Lubin informs Dandin of Angélique's infidelity (which he already vaguely suspected), his reaction is — again — to compare his real fate as the husband of a noble girl and the fate he might (and should) have had by marrying a peasant. His second monologue (I:3) explicitly compares two systems of values and manners. An "egalitarian" peasant marriage preserves the desirable hierarchy between husband and wife and authorizes immediate and brutal male domination: the husband, master in his own house, can "faire justice à bons coups de bâton" ("settle the matter to [his] satisfaction by giving her a sound beating"). An "unequal" alliance confuses the natural distribution of authority, forces the husband to delegate the enforcement of justice to others, and excludes all physical violence. Literally as well as figuratively, Dandin's "hands are tied" by a social obligation that forbids him the usual behaviors of his culture (or at least, forbids him the acts assigned to peasants by theatrical convention). A "disproportionate" marriage brings a twofold disorder: Dandin must give up the husband's usual power of justice over his wife and himself become the solicitor, begging reparation of his injustice. And in order to do so, he must exhibit his misfortune, make it known, render it public, rather than (as was customary) hide it from the eyes of society.

By having his character express a nostalgia for frank violence and regret that he cannot use a legitimate brutality, Molière tears him asunder between two sorts of "habitus": obliged to submit to the rules of noble marriage alliance, Dandin cannot act as a peasant would, and, as a peasant, he has not internalized the codes and controls characteristic of aristocratic behavior. Furetière's *Dictionnaire* gives as an illustration of *civilité*, "Peasants lack civility," thus recalling a commonplace of his age and one Molière manipulates with particular acuity. Physical violence, in act or in imagination, is the clearest indication of behavior that lacks self-control (is not *policé*) and is not civil (*civilisé*); it is symptomatic of a "rusticity" that the dictionaries of the age present as the antonym of *civilité*.

*   *   *

Thus Dandin is a character who speaks to us of how identity is constructed, of the impossibility of changing one's social status, and of the mechanisms that regulate social classification. At the same time, he is also a character made ridiculous by his outlandish costume, his foolish name, and his country bumpkin's fancies. How was this mixture of qualities — which is precisely what has given rise to contradictory readings of the play — received by spectators of the play in 1668? On what common horizon of thoughts and intellectual acquisitions, broad or narrow, was the comedy inscribed? *George Dandin* is *une farce pour rire*. Granted. But just what was the network of connivances between Molière and his public that also made it decipherable as the bearer of a message on what society was or should be? Was it the verisimilitude of Dandin's situation, rare but not impossible? But in 1668 peasants were no more likely to marry the daughters of gentlefolk than princes were to marry shepherdesses. What I want to stress is that no one — either at the court or in Paris — would have been able to believe in the reality of such an alliance, which means that from the outset the plot was classified as parody. If one eyewitness could qualify the play as *archi-comique*, it is perhaps primarily because the basic situation that it represented was so absurd, so incongruous, that laughter was the only possible reaction.

Laughter, because Dandin picked the wrong century. It was not unknown in France for wealthy peasants, farmers or husbandmen, to become the equals of the gentlemen in their village, and even to enter into the nobility if they acquired a fief and took on a noble lifestyle — but only before the mid-sixteenth century.[44] After 1560, that sort of ambition was no longer possible. For one thing, royal decrees rejected such ennoblements as "false nobility." The decree of 1579 specifies that "the commoners and non-nobles who buy noble fiefs will not be ennobled by that fact no matter what the revenues of the fiefs they have acquired." For another, the gentry would no longer accept as peers people who imitated their lifestyle without proper title to it. Like Don Quixote, Dandin suffers under the effects of *hysteresis*: he is unable to recognize that the mechanisms from which he hopes to profit no longer exist. Furthermore, the way in which he hopes to gain equality with the nobles is socially impossible (and was impossible even in the sixteenth century). He wants it immediately, whereas when a family was integrated into the second estate it always presupposed a long process of assimilation and gradual recognition. He wants it on the land, with no urban stage, whereas the usual route to ennoblement for a family of peasant origins had always led to the city and to earning bourgeois notability, exercising a profession in the law and buying an office.[45]

Dandin also elicited laughter because nobles — even "poor" nobles, even nobles plagued with debts — did not marry their daughters to simple

peasants, even wealthy ones. Misalliances did exist, and were even more numerous after 1660, probably because of the financial difficulties that some
(and only some) aristocratic families experienced. Never, though, in the
cases that have been studied, did such difficulties authorize a peasant to
become part of a gentleman's family. The "elect" who did so were of a quite
different social status, marked by the possession of an office, royal or seigneurial, or at the least by a solid bourgeois status that supposed an independent income unsullied by "mechanical" labor or any economically productive activity.[46] The spectators of 1668 would have automatically considered
the notion of a peasant married to a noble unbelievable and the peasant's
claim that he should be taken as the equal of gentlefolk senseless. The
perception of society of those audiences — their "social acumen" — necessarily included a feeling for what was socially possible or impossible. One of
the strongest "connivances" between Molière and his audience was taking
that spontaneous and broadly shared social knowledge for granted. There
was no need to state it explicitly. Fully as much as identification by genre
and form, that social sense gives meaning to a work by providing a standard
by which to gauge the sort of relationship that the play establishes with the
social world. Here it indicated that the situation was fantastic, imagined for
the stage but unimaginable in the reality of the social relations of the time.

Is this to say that Félibien was off the mark when he commented on the
comedy as a natural, true-to-life, even true "representation"? And is it to say
that the spectators could see nothing in the play that bore any relation to the
organization of their own society? On 18 July at Versailles, Abbé de Montigny noted the presence of Madame and Mademoiselle de Sévigné among
the ladies admitted to the king's table. Unfortunately, Madame de Sévigné
said nothing about the festivities or about the comedy. Her letters during
the summer of 1668 are completely taken up by her quarrel with Bussy-
Rabutin about a portrait of her that he had published and that was not to
her liking, and also about the reform of the nobility of Champagne.[47]

The reform that so preoccupied Madame de Sévigné in the summer of
1668 aimed at verifying the nobility of families who claimed noble status
and rejecting as commoners all who could not offer written proof of at least
four degrees (that is, generations in the male line) of nobility. The reform,
which began in the aftermath of the Fronde, received vigorous support
from a declaration of the king dated 8 February 1661. Between that date and
1668, twenty-five legislative and regulatory texts stipulated procedures for
researching degrees of nobility and extended the researchers' powers. Standards were rigorous, since a minimum of three documents had to be pro-

duced in proof of each degree of nobility to attest that the persons involved were exempt from the *taille* and that they lived in a noble style. Acceptable proofs included mentions of *noble homme* or *écuyer* in notarial acts (such as marriage contracts, acts of guardianship, or acts confirming land sales); *aveux et dénobrements* (acts of recognition between vassal and suzerain or between peasant and lord); mentions in the official records of the Cour des Aides; or genealogies drawn up and certified during earlier reforms.[48] The prime reason for these searches was, of course, fiscal, since anyone who fell short was subject to payment of the *taille*. But they also were aimed at preventing too easy an access to nobility, something that a mercantile society saw as a mortal peril because it reduced the number of both taxpayers and productive persons, by that token reducing the wealth, and thus the power, of the state. Beyond such considerations, however, the reform aimed at restoring order to society by designating as authentically noble only those persons who could prove nobility by submitting written proof and by an appeal to history. For the king, the intendants, the officials of the tax office, and the tax farmers who carried on the verifications, social rank could no longer be determined by the will of individuals, even those who could support their claims with a certain number of visible signs of nobility such as a noble lifestyle and the possession of seigneurial lands. Basically, rank depended on a recognition of written documents on the part of authority, which had the power to pass on the true social status of its own subjects. And was not the relationship between those subjects and their sovereign analogous to the relationship Molière establishes between the peasant who thinks himself the equal of a gentleman and the gentleman who declares that he is not?

In any event, it is probable that the court saw the play with some thought of these reforms that were agitating and exciting all the nobility of the kingdom. "I am obsessed with this folly," Madame de Sévigné wrote. Molière himself makes the connection in a detail of his play: Dandin's mother-in-law, Madame de la Prudoterie, declares that she herself was born into a "family whose nobility passes through the distaff side, through which your children, by this great privilege, will become gentry." Some provinces, Champagne and neighboring districts in particular, had customary laws that recognized that a noble woman married to a commoner could transmit her nobility to her children. It was a point that was hotly debated during reforms of the nobility. The tax farmers who were charged with verification (and who had a personal interest in increasing the number of rejections, since their living came from tax collection) denied the validity of that "uterine nobility" and considered the children born of marriages between noble-women and commoner husbands to be commoners. The nobility of Champagne defended the rights of "maternal nobility," and the King's Council admitted their claims and ordered the tax farmers to cease and desist.[49] This dispute was one of the chief preoccupations of the nobility in the 1660s. Molière makes use of it, clearly linking the plot of his comedy to the research into family nobility that followed the royal declaration of 1661. La Bruyère hints at the same controversy in his *Characters* when he exclaims, "How many children would welcome a law that decreed that the womb ennobles! But how many others would suffer from it."[50]

For the courtiers who attended the performance in 1668, *George Dandin* might have been interpreted as a text that made use of a totally imaginary plot to evoke the major question facing the nobility of France: how, and by whom, is social identity defined? On the stage, the gentleman decides the social identity of a peasant who cannot accept the image of himself that others present to him. But in the society of the real world, a noble was forced to accept what someone else said that he was or was not. For him as for Dandin, the way he perceives himself and classifies himself is meaningless if it lacks the legitimacy accorded by a prince who can declare who has usurped his title and who has not, who belongs to the second estate and who is to be cut out of it. When documentation was convincing, verification could involve a self-satisfied ostentation. Madame de Sévigné reported:

> We had to show our nobility in Brittany, and those who had the most of it took pleasure in making the best of the occasion to display all their merchandise. Here is ours: fourteen marriage contracts from father to son; three hundred fifty years of knighthood; ancestors often considerable in the wars of Brittany and prominent in history; at times, great wealth, at other times less, but always good and grand alliances.[51]

But the reform reminded even the families who were sure of their titles of nobility and took pride in them that their identity depended on a sovereign judgment; it alone could say whether their social being conformed to the monarchy's definition of the noble condition. At court *George Dandin* may thus have been understood as a text that spoke of a true social situation, not the absurd fiction played out on the stage, but the situation of all the gentlefolk whose status was identified and certified by the royal decision. For them the relationship between society and the comic text, rather than lying in any possible similarity in situation, could be found in an exhibition, by analogy and shifted out of phase, of the very principle governing the definition of all social identity, including their own. This means that a strong connection was established between the plot of the comedy, which showed an impossible usurpation of status,[52] and the circumstances in which it was performed, which celebrated the absolute power of the king.

The Paris audience, nearly all commoners and in the majority bourgeois (in the broader sense of the term), probably did not attend the comedy with any idea in mind of proofs of nobility, hardly among their concerns. The story had another sense for its city spectators, and it played on another law of the workings of society. Félibien suggests a reading of that sort when he gives universal scope to the peasant Dandin's woes: "Nothing could be more true to life than what [Molière] has done to show the anguish and the vexations often experienced by those who marry above their station." The remark takes on the tone of a lesson arguing in favor of social endogamy and, beyond that, for continuity of familial status. In the latter half of the seventeenth century, social mobility from the third to the second estate was usually thought of as a disorder that upset natural hierarchies, confused established relationships, and threatened political order. Bourgeois who aspired to becoming gentlemen were shown in the theater as ridiculous or dupes because they perturbed a social equilibrium in which each person had been put in his proper place (or returned to it). In such a society, legitimate chances for rising from the third estate to the second had become strictly codified and were few and far between. Making people laugh at those who, in spite of such difficulties, tried to break through the barriers separating orders and estates was perhaps a way to defuse unwelcome attempts to do just that. The spectators at the Palais Royal must have sensed that the comedy, under the guise of showing a peasant in a farce, carried a warning against unwarranted ambitions and a message in support of an order in which everyone stayed in his place. In the long run, whether Molière subscribed to that ideology is not of much importance. The task of the play is not to preach a social morality; it shows, in an imaginary situation, the effects of an illusory belief in social mobility. This is where it may have met the horizon of beliefs of the Paris spectators, many of whom, on all levels of the social hierarchy, may have shared the perception of the social world that underlay Dandin's foolish hopes. The fictional plot suggested to them that it would be a good idea to get rid of such notions, especially in an age that proclaimed the ideal of unchanging status, where hierarchies were clearly delineated and people of different social status were kept firmly separated.

But did they get the message? Perhaps, perhaps not. The ambiguous subtlety of Molière's caricature of Dandin consists in preserving, within a possible universal application, another reading that sees in Dandin nothing but the ridicule of excess. The Paris audience — commoners and bourgeois, petty or grand — probably understood that the comedy touched on a fundamental tension between an aspiration for personal or familial social promotion (which they shared) and a much-reiterated norm that worked to immobilize and reproduce the existing social order. The Paris audience may have understood the play as a warning for everyone, whatever the person's social rank and level of ambition. But it may also have seen nothing in the comedy but Dandin's outlandish exaggeration, which might reinforce belief that a more reasonable ambition would succeed. The "universality" of Molière is a classic literary commonplace, but its validity lies in this plurality of possible receptions of a work that uses situations far removed from the order of the socially possible to lay bare the very real principles of how society operates.

4. Popular Appropriations: The Readers and Their Books

Popular culture is a category of the learned. Why should I begin with such an abrupt proposition? Simply to remind us that the debates surrounding even the definition of popular culture engage a concept that attempts to define, characterize and name practices never designated by their actors as part of "popular culture." An intellectual category aiming to encompass and describe artifacts and behaviors situated outside learned culture, the concept of popular culture, in its multiple and contradictory meanings, has expressed the relationships maintained by western intellectuals (among them "scholars") with those whose cultural otherness is even more difficult to understand than that encountered in "exotic" lands.

Risking extreme simplification, one can reduce the innumerable definitions of popular culture to two great descriptive and interpretive models. The first, aiming to abolish all forms of cultural ethnocentrism, conceives of popular culture as a coherent and autonomous symbolic system that functions according to a logic absolutely foreign to those of literate culture. The second, concerned with emphasizing the relations of domination that organize the social world, perceives popular culture in its dependencies and deficiencies with respect to the dominant culture. On one side, then, popular culture constitutes a world apart, closed on itself, independent. On the other, popular culture is completely defined by its distance from a cultural legitimacy of which it is deprived.

With strategies of research, styles of description, and theoretical propositions completely opposed, these two models have penetrated all the disciplines engaged in research into popular culture: history, anthropology, and sociology. Jean-Claude Passeron has recently shown the methodological dangers of both of these models:

> Just as the sociological blindness of cultural relativism applied to popular cultures encourages *populisme*, according to which popular practices are carried out completely in the monadic happiness of symbolic autosufficiency, so the

> theory of cultural legitimacy risks . . . leading to *légitimisme* which, in the
> extreme form of *misérabilisme*, does nothing more than discount in sorrow
> differences as deficiencies, otherness as a lesser form of existence.[1]

The opposition holds true term for term: the celebration of a majestic popular culture opposes a description "by default"; the recognition of equal dignity in all the symbolic universes opposes a reminder of the implacable hierarchies of the social world.

One might follow Passeron when he remarks that as these definitions of popular culture are logically and methodologically contradictory, they do not serve as adequate principles of classification for scholarship: "the oscillation between these two ways of describing popular culture can be found in the same work, in the same author" and their boundary "runs sinuously in all descriptions of popular culture that combine these alternative interpretive strategies."[2]

As a historian, I might add that the contrast between these two perspectives — that which accents the symbolic autonomy of popular culture and that which insists on its dependence with respect to the dominant culture — is the foundation of all chronological models that oppose a golden age of popular culture, original and independent, to a time of censure and constraints that disqualified and dismantled it.

We must be careful not to accept without reservation the now-consecrated time scheme that considers the first half of the seventeenth century in Western Europe to have been a period of major rupture that pitted a golden age of vibrant, free, and profuse popular culture against an age of church and state discipline that repressed and subjugated that culture. According to this view, after 1600 or 1650 the combined efforts of the repressive churches of the Protestant and Catholic Reformations to "acculturate" the population, and those of the absolutist states to centralize and unify the nation, are seen as stifling or inhibiting the inventive exuberance of an ancient culture. By imposing new discipline, by inculcating a new submissiveness, by teaching new models of comportment, church and state allegedly destroyed the roots and ancient equilibrium of a traditional way of viewing and experiencing the world. "Popular culture, as much rural as urban, experienced an almost complete eclipse in the era of the Sun King. Its internal coherence disappeared definitively. It could no longer be a system of survival, a philosophy of existence," writes Robert Muchembled in his description of the "repression of popular culture" in France during the seventeenth and eighteenth centuries.[3]

In a more subtle way, Peter Burke describes the two movements that have altered traditional popular culture: on one hand, a systematic attempt by some of the educated, mostly Catholic and Protestant clergy, "to change the attitudes and values of the rest of the population" and "to suppress, or at least purify, many items of traditional popular culture," and on the other hand, the withdrawal of the upper classes from popular culture. The result is clear:

> In 1500, popular culture was everyone's culture; a second culture for the educated, and the only culture for everybody else. By 1800, however, in most parts of Europe, the clergy, the nobility, the merchants, the professional men — and their wives — had abandoned popular culture to the lower classes, from whom they were now separated, as never before, by profound differences in world view."[4]

There are several reasons to be skeptical about such a time scheme. First, it is apparent that when this scheme contrasts the splendor of the culture of the people on one side of a watershed with misery on the other, it reiterates for the early modern period an opposition that historians or sociologists have seen in other ages. In like fashion, in the thirteenth century, a reordering of the theological, scientific, and philosophical domains that separated learned culture from the folk tradition resulted in the censure of practices henceforth held to be superstitious or heterodox. If Jacques Le Goff recognizes in the twelfth century "the growth of a lay popular culture, rushing into the breach opened . . . by a lay aristocratic culture thoroughly imbued with the one available culture system distinct from the clergy's, namely, the tradition of folklore,"[5] for Jean-Claude Schmitt the thirteenth century opens a real "acculturation":

> One must wonder if the growing suspicion directed against folk practices of the body (dance, for example), the personalizing of experience always urged in sermons due to the generalization of the sacrament of penitence . . . , [and] the institution in the fifteenth century of a religious education beginning in childhood (see Gerson), have not jointly contributed to internalize the sense of sin and to make all people feel guilt, blinding them to the "acculturation" which they underwent in being convinced of the immorality of their own culture.[6]

A similar cultural watershed is supposed to have occurred in France during the half-century that separated the wars of 1870 and 1914, a period devoted to freeing traditional cultures — peasant and "popular" — from their enclaves (thus uprooting them) and to promoting a unified, national, and republican culture of modern stamp.[7] Another such transformation is assumed to have occurred before and after the advent of contemporary mass culture, which, in this view, has used the new media to destroy an ancient, creative, plural, and free culture. Historiographically speaking, therefore, the fate of popular culture seems forever to be stifled, inhibited, and abraded, but at the same time ever to be reborn out of its decay. This indicates, perhaps, that the true problem is not to identify the decisive moment of the disappearance of popular culture, but rather to consider for each epoch how complex relations were developed between forms imposed (more or less forcibly) and established practices (sometimes allowed to blossom and sometimes restrained).

This leads to yet another reason for not organizing our entire description of the cultures of the European ancien régime according to the rupture that is generally agreed to have taken place in the seventeenth century (earlier in some places, later in others). In point of fact, no matter how forcefully cultural models may have been imposed, they might nevertheless have been received with reactions that varied from mistrust to outright rebellion. A description of the norms, disciplines, discourses, and teachings through which absolutist, Reformation culture may have intended to subject the population does not prove that the people were in fact totally and universally subjected. To the contrary, we should assume that a gap existed between the norm and real-life experience, between injunction and practice, and between the sense intended and the sense constructed — a gap into which reformulations and procedures for avoidance could flow. The culture imposed by those in power during those centuries was no more able than the more powerful mass culture of our times to destroy the particular identities and deep-rooted practices that resisted it. What changed in our era, obviously, was the manner in which those identities and practices were expressed and by which they affirmed their existence and made their own use of innovations originally designed to curtail them. But accepting this mutation as incontestable does not necessarily oblige us to acknowledge a rupture in cultural continuity throughout the three centuries of the early modern period. Nor does it force us to agree that, after a turning point, there was no place left for practices and thoughts other than those that churchmen, the servants of the state, or the makers of discourses wanted to inculcate.

*   *   *

These are, it seems to me, questions of the same order as those posed in Lawrence W. Levine's thesis of "cultural bifurcation" to characterize the trajectory of American culture in the nineteenth century. It rests on a major chronological contrast, opposing an ancient time of sharing, mixing, and cultural exuberance with a new separation between publics, spaces, genres, styles:

> Everywhere in the society of the second half of the nineteenth century American culture was undergoing a process of fragmentation. . . . It was manifest in the relative decline of a shared public culture which in the second half of the nineteenth century fractured into a series of discrete cultures that had less and less to do one with another. Theaters, opera houses, museums, auditoriums that had once housed mixed crowds of people experiencing an eclectic blend of expressive culture were increasingly filtering their clientele and their programs so that less and less could one find audiences that cut across the social and economic spectrum enjoying an expressive culture which blended together mixed elements of what we would today call high, low, and folk culture.[8]

A double evolution leads from the "shared public culture" to the "bifurcated culture": on one hand, a process of retreat and subtraction, which assigns to cultural practices a distinctive value all the more powerful as they are less shared; on the other hand, a process of disqualification and exclusion that rejects as outside of a sacred, canonical culture the works, objects, and forms henceforth dismissed as popular.

This model is strikingly similar to that used to describe the cultural trajectory of western societies between the sixteenth and eighteenth centuries. Here, too, a cultural bifurcation, instigated by the retreat of elites and the isolation of popular culture into its own separate sphere, dislocates a longstanding common base — the "Bakhtinian," folkloric, festive, and carnivalesque culture of the public square. In both cases the same questions could be posed. Was this original shared culture really so homogeneous? And during the period of separation and differentiation, were the boundaries between legitimate and disqualified culture really so distinct and watertight? For nineteenth-century America, David D. Hall responds negatively to these two questions: on the one hand, the "shared public culture" of the first half of the nineteenth century is not free of exclusions and social cleavages; on the other, the "commodification" of the symbolic goods apparently most alien to the market and the capture by commercial culture of the signs and values of legitimate culture involves powerful exchanges between the literate and the popular.[9]

Another question is that of the chronology of these two trajectories, European and American. Must we assume that one or two centuries later American culture traveled the same road as that of old regime societies in

Western Europe? Or, on the contrary, should we assume that the cultural evolution of the second half of the nineteenth century — in which elites scorned a popular culture identified with commodified culture — were identical on the whole throughout a Western world unified by trans-Atlantic migrations? No doubt the connection is strong between the reclamation, on one hand, of a "pure" or "purified" culture — distanced from vulgar tastes, removed from laws of economic production, and carried by the aesthetic complicity between creators and their public — with, on the other hand, the conquests of commercial culture, dominated by capitalist enterprise and addressed to the widest possible audience. As Pierre Bourdieu has shown recently, the establishment in France during the second half of the nineteenth century of a literary field defined as a world apart, founded on the autonomy, disinterestedness, and absolute liberty of aesthetic creation, was directly tied to the rejection of "industrial literature" for its servitude to popular preferences that determined its success:

> The relationship of writers and artists to the market, whose anonymous sanction might create unprecedented disparities between them, contributes, no doubt, to the ambivalent representation of the "great public," at once fascinating and scorned, in which is mixed both the "bourgeois," enslaved to the vulgar concerns of business, and the "people," abandoned to the stultification of productive activities.[10]

*   *   *

For a long time the dominant and classical understanding of popular culture in Europe and perhaps in America was founded on three assumptions: first, that popular culture can be defined in contrast to what it is not; second, that it is possible to characterize as popular the public of particular cultural productions; and third, that cultural artifacts can be considered as socially pure, as popular in and of themselves. These three characteristics are central, for example, in the classic works done in France on "popular literature," chapbooks sold by peddlers, or "popular religion," the set of beliefs and practices considered a constituent part of a religion of the masses.

But according to more recent work on both topics the assumptions that had defined popular culture are dubious. "Popular literature" and "popular religion" were not radically different from the literature of the elites or the religion of the clerics; they were shared by social groups not exclusively popular; they were at the same time acculturated and acculturating.

Consequently, I have argued that it is pointless to try to identify popular culture by some supposedly specific distribution of cultural objects or models. Their distribution is always more complex than it might seem at first glance, as are their uses by groups or individuals. A sociology implying that the classification of social groups corresponds strictly to a classification of cultural products or practices can no longer be accepted uncritically. It is clear that the appropriation of texts, codes, or values in a given society may be a more distinctive factor than the always illusory correspondence between a series of cultural artifacts and a specific socio-cultural level. The "popular" cannot be found ready-made in a set of texts or habits that merely need to be identified, listed, and described. Above all, the "popular" can indicate a kind of relation, a way of using cultural products or norms that are shared, more or less, by society at large, but understood, defined, and used in styles that vary. Such an argument evidently changes the work of the historian or sociologist because it requires identifying and distinguishing not cultural sets defined in themselves as popular, but rather the ways in which common cultural sets are appropriated differently.

Thus it seems necessary to place the notion of appropriation at the center of a cultural historical approach. Focusing on differentiated practices and contrasted uses of the same texts, codes, or models, this concept allows us to overcome the dichotomy between the two definitions of popular culture: popular culture as a completely autonomous symbolic world, and popular culture as molded and manipulated by high culture. I propose a reformulation of the concept of appropriation that accentuates plural uses and diverse understandings and diverges from the meaning Michel Foucault gives appropriation when he holds "the social appropriation of discourse" to be one of the primary procedures for gaining control of discourses and putting them beyond the reach of those who were denied access to them.[11] It also parts company with the meaning hermeneutics gives to appropriation, which is identified with the process of (postulated as universal) interpretation.[12] In my own perspective, appropriation involves a social history of the various uses (which are not necessarily interpretations) of discourses and models, brought back to their fundamental social and institutional determinants and lodged in the specific practices that produce them. To concentrate on the concrete conditions and processes that construct meaning is to recognize, unlike traditional intellectual history, that minds are not disincarnated, and, unlike hermeneutics, that the categories which engender experiences and interpretations are historical, discontinuous, and differentiated.

If it permits us to break with an illusory definition of popular culture, the notion of appropriation might also reintroduce another illusion: the illusion that considers the variety of cultural practices to be a neutral system of differences, an ensemble of diverse but equivalent practices. Such a perspective would ignore the fact that symbolic goods are always the object of social conflict over their classification, hierarchization, and consecration or disqualification. To understand "popular culture" is, therefore, to situate within this arena of confrontation the knotty relationships between, on one hand, the mechanisms of symbolic domination that aim to make the dominated themselves accept the very representations that qualify (or, rather, disqualify) their culture as "popular," and, on the other hand, the specific logic at work in the customs, practices, and ways of making one's own that which is imposed.

A precious resource for understanding this tension (and for avoiding the oscillation between those approaches that insist on the dependence of popular culture and those that exalt its autonomy) is furnished by the distinction between strategy and tactic as formulated by de Certeau. Strategies involve places and institutions; they produce objects, norms, or models; they accumulate and capitalize. Tactics, deprived of a proper place and without mastery over time, are "ways of doing," or better yet, "of doing with." "Popular" forms of culture, from daily practices to cultural consumption, might be thought of as tactics that construct meaning — but meaning possibly foreign to that originally intended:

> To a rationalized, expansionist and at the same time centralized, clamorous, and spectacular production corresponds *another* production, called "consumption." The latter is devious, it is dispersed, but it insinuates itself everywhere, silently and almost invisibly, because it does not manifest itself through its own products, but rather through its *ways of using* the products imposed by a dominant economic order.[13]

*   *   *

This perspective profoundly transforms our understanding of a practice at once exemplary and central: reading. Apparently passive and submissive, reading is, in fact, in its own way, inventive and creative. With respect to contemporary society, de Certeau has superbly underlined this paradox:

> Reading (an image or a text) seems to constitute the maximal development of the passivity assumed to characterize the consumer, who is conceived as a voyeur (whether troglodytic or itinerant) in a "show biz society." In reality, the activity of reading has on the contrary all the characteristics of a silent produc-

tion: the drift across the page, the metamorphosis of the text effected by the wandering eyes of the reader, the improvisation and expectations of meanings inferred from a few words, leaps over written space in an ephemeral dance. . . . [The reader] insinuates into another person's text the ruses of pleasures and appropriation: he poaches on it, is transported into it, pluralizes himself in it.[14]

This image of the reader poaching on a text that is not his own raises a fundamental question of all cultural history or sociology: that of the variation, according to time and place, of social groups and "interpretive communities," of the conditions of possibility, and of the methods and effects of this poaching. For England in the 1950s, Richard Hoggart characterizes the popular reading of widely circulated songs, advertisements, horoscopes, and romances as reading that made for belief and disbelief, that encouraged belief in what was read (or heard) without completely eliminating distance and doubts as to its authenticity.[15] The "oblique" attention is one of the keys to an understanding of just how the culture of the popular classes can distance itself, make a place for itself, or establish its own coherence in the models imposed upon it through force or persuasion by dominant groups or powers. Such a perspective provides a counterweight to an emphasis on the discursive or institutional apparatus in a society that is designed to discipline bodies and practices and shape conduct and thought. The determination to impose cultural models on the people does not guarantee the way in which they are used, adapted, understood.

Janice A. Radway reaches similar conclusions in her meticulous study of the appropriation by a particular "interpretive community" (in this case, a community of female readers) of a genre of "mass-market publishing," the "romance":

Commodities like mass-produced literary texts are selected, purchased, constructed, and used by real people with previously existing needs, desires, intentions, and interpretive strategies. By reinstating those active individuals and their creative, constructive activities at the heart of our interpretive enterprise, we avoid blinding ourselves to the fact that the essentially human practice of making meaning goes on even in a world increasingly dominated by things and by consumption. In thus recalling the interactive character of operations like reading . . . we increase our chances of sorting out or articulating the difference between the repressive imposition of ideology and oppositional practices that, though limited in their scope and effect, at least dispute or contest the control of ideological forms.[16]

If "opportunities still exist within the mass-communication process for individuals to resist, alter, and reappropriate the materials designed elsewhere for their purchase,"[17] it would lead us to assume, a fortiori, that similar possibilities were offered to readers of societies of the ancien régime, in an era when the control of models transmitted by print was (except for particular situations) less complete than that of the twentieth century. One must challenge, therefore, any approach claiming that the repertoire of the literature of colportage expressed the *mentalité* or the "world view" of popular readers. Such an argument, commonly found in works on the French *Bibliothèque bleue*, the English chapbooks, or the Castilian and Catalan *pliegos sueltos*, is no longer acceptable. There are several reasons for this: because texts published in the books and booklets of colportage belong to multiple and fragmented genres, eras and traditions; because over the centuries the chronological and social distance was often great between the context of the production and that of the reception of these texts; because as always, a gap separates what is proposed by the text and what is made of it by the reader. Proof can be found in texts that, once in printed form, entered into the repertoire of the *Bibliothèque bleue*. Literate in origin and belonging to diverse genres, they reached, thanks to their new printed form—that of inexpensive editions—and their mode of distribution—colportage—audiences very different from those that made their first success, and, because of this, they were invested with meanings far removed from those originally intended.

To consider the relation between texts of colportage and the social world of ancien régime societies is to assume two complementary procedures. The first, reversing ordinarily recognized causalities, suggests an interpretation of "popular literature" as a repertoire of models of comportment, as an ensemble of representations of imitable (and possibly imitated) norms. The second centers on the variety and instability of meanings assigned to the same text by different audiences. We must not posit an equivalence between the repertoire of colportage and "popular *mentalité*," which risks being a mere tautology (since the success of "popular literature" is explained by its resemblance to a *mentalité* that, in fact, is deduced from the very themes of the books). Instead, what is called for is a social history of the uses and understandings of texts by communities of readers who, successively, take possession of them. Numerous and complex mediations must take place between texts that become "steady sellers" in colportage and the meanings invested in them in different historical situations and for different readers.

We must recognize, therefore, a major tension between the explicit or implicit intentions a text proposes to a wide audience and the variety of possible reading responses. The printed works designed for "popular" consumption in early modern Europe reveal a broad range of intentions: Christianizing, as in the texts of Counter-Reformation devotion that entered into the French *Bibliothèque bleue*; reformist, as in the almanacs of the German *Volksauflärung*; didactic, as in material printed for scholarly use and manuals of practical instruction; parodic, as in texts in the picaresque and burlesque traditions; poetic, as in the *romances* published in the Castilian *pliegos*. But in their reception (certainly difficult for the historian to decipher) these texts were often understood and handled by their "popular" readers without regard for the intentions that governed their production or distribution. Either readers took as imaginary that which had been intended for utilitarian instruction, or, conversely, they understood fictions as realistic descriptions. The collections of epistolary models in the *Bibliothèque bleue*—all taken from court literature of the early seventeenth century and reedited for a wide audience from the mid-seventeenth century to the beginning of the nineteenth century—illustrate the first case: deprived of all utility for readers who never found themselves in a situation to use the models proposed, they were undoubtedly read as fictive stories, as rudimentary outlines of epistolary novels.[18] The repertoire of picaresque literature in the same series presents an opposite situation: playing with carnivalesque, parodic, and burlesque conventions and references, they might well have been understood as truthfully describing the troubling and strange reality of false beggars and real thieves.[19]

This leads to an important difference between readers of the ancien régime and the female readers of romance novels questioned by Janice A. Radway or the readers in New South Wales interviewed by Martyn Lyons and Lucy Taksa.[20] Readers of the *Bibliothèque bleue* and other European literatures of colportage have, with rare exceptions, said nothing of their readings—or at least nothing conserved for the historian. To describe popular uses of texts and books is, therefore, no easy task. Such descriptions must rely on sources that are always representations of reading: iconographic depictions of the circumstances of reading and of the objects read;[21] representations of reading and writing practices in the stories, manuals, calendars, or almanacs intended for a "popular" market; representations of the competencies and expectations of the least capable readers, such as are implied in the physical forms of colportage editions;[22] and less often, representations of their own reading by plebian or peasant readers in autobiographical writing[23] or when an authority (ecclesiastical or inquisitorial, for example) requires them to explain how they came upon and understood the books they read.[24] When we are confronted with these texts and images that bring popular readers into our view, caution is indispensable. Whatever they might be, these representations never involve immediate and transparent relations with the practices they describe. All are lodged in the specific modes of their production, the interests and intentions that produced them, the genres in which they were inscribed, and the audiences at which they were aimed. To reconstruct the conventions that governed literate representations of the popular, therefore, we must decipher the strong but subtle bond that ties these representations to the social practices that are their object.

Acknowledging these complexities, an understanding of popular readers in ancien régime societies might begin with the great morphological oppositions that govern the transmission of texts — those, for example, between reading out loud and reading silently, or between reading and recitation. This last contrast is particularly pertinent for societies where orality holds an essential place. On one hand, it designates the possible submission of printed texts to procedures proper to oral "performance." If, in France, the reading aloud of colportage books at the *veillée* (evening gathering) is attested to only rarely before the second half of the nineteenth century, their "declamation" — that is, their knowledge by heart and their restoration in a living utterance, detached from a reading of texts and resembling a recitation of tales — was a major form of their transmission and one source of variants that modify the printed texts. On the other hand, the circulation of the printed repertoire affects oral traditions, which are profoundly contaminated and transformed (as is shown by the example of fairy tales) by literate and learned versions of traditional stories, such as those widely diffused by the literature of colportage.[25]

To attach the category "popular" to ways of reading, and not to specific texts, is both essential and risky. After Carlo Ginzburg's exemplary study, the temptation is strong to understand popular reading in the early modern period through the example of Menocchio — that is, as a discontinuous process that dismembers texts, decontextualizes words and sentences, and assumes a literal meaning.[26] Such a diagnosis seems confirmed by analyses of the textual and material structure of printed works intended for the widest audiences; they were organized in brief and disjointed sequences, sealed upon themselves, and repetitive, apparently adapted to readers whose memory retained only fragments of the text.

However important, this perspective must be qualified. Are not the reading practices described thus far as specifically popular and rooted in an ancient oral and peasant culture also those, in different forms, of literate people during the same time period? The two emblematic objects of learned readership in the Renaissance — the book wheel, which permitted the opening of several books at a time, and thus the extraction and comparison of passages taken as essential, and the commonplace book, which collected citations, examples, sentences, and experiences — also imply a readership that cuts up, fragments, decontextualizes, and invests an absolute authority in the literal meaning of the written word.[27]

The identification of morphological traits that organize reading practices is therefore necessary but not sufficient to describe cultural differences adequately. Popular forms of practices are not deployed in a separate and specific symbolic universe; their difference is always constructed by way of mediations and dependencies that tie them to dominant models and norms.

*   *   *

In our current intellectual debates, the approach for which we have argued — defining cultural configurations ("popular" or not) by starting with practice, and, therefore, with modes of appropriation — faces two dangers. The first is the "linguistic turn" or the "semiotic challenge" addressing textual criticism and the social sciences. We see here three base principles: to take language as a closed system of signs whose relations automatically produce meaning; to consider the construction of signification as detached from all intention and all subjective control; and to take reality as constituted by language itself, independent of all objective reference. John E. Toews has summarized clearly this radical position, which assumes that "language is conceived as a self-contained system of 'signs' whose meanings are determined by their relations to each other rather than by their relations to some 'transcendental' or extralinguistic object or subject," and postulates that "the creation of meaning is impersonal, operating 'behind the backs' of language users whose linguistic actions can merely exemplify the rules and the procedures of languages they inhabit but do not control."[28]

Against these radical formulations, we must, I believe, remember that it is not acceptable to impose the logic that governs the production of discourses on practices constitutive of the social world. To affirm that reality is accessible only by way of discourses (and for the historian these discourses are almost always written texts) that desire to organize, represent, or subdue it is not, for all that, to postulate an identity between the logo-

centric and hermeneutic logic that governs the production of these discourses and the "logic of practice" that rules behaviors that define social
identities and relations. All cultural analysis must take into account this
irreducibility of experience to discourse. It must guard against an uncon-
trolled use of the category of the text, against applying the notion of the text
to practices (ordinary or ritual) whose tactics and procedures are not at all
similar to strategies that produce discourses. To maintain such a distinction
is essential in order to avoid, as Bourdieu says, "giving as the principle for
the practices of individuals the theory that one must construct in order to
explain them," or even to give "to a practice a function which is not the
function for its actors, but rather for those who study this practice as a thing
to be deciphered."[29]

Moreover, the fundamental object of a history, or of a cultural sociology understood as the history of the construction of meaning, resides in the
tension between the inventive capacities of individuals or communities and
the constraints, norms, and conventions that limit — more or less forcibly
according to their position in the relations of domination — what is possible
for them to think, to express, to do. This perspective is valuable for a history
of literate works, always inscribed into the field of the possible that renders
them thinkable. It is also valuable for a history of practices that are also
inventions of meanings limited by the multiple determinants (social, religious, institutional, etc.) that define for each community acceptable behavior and internalized norms. To the automatic and impersonal nature of
the production of meaning as postulated by the "linguistic turn," we must
oppose another perspective, which insists upon the culturally and socially
determined freedoms that these "interstices inherent in the general system
of norms (or the contradictions between them) leave to actors."[30]

The second danger resides in the implicit definitions of a category like
"popular culture." Whether one intends it or not, the very term implies that
the culture it designates is as autonomous as distant, "exotic" cultures and is
located symmetrically in respect to the dominant, literate, elite culture. We
must dispel these complementary illusions. On one hand, popular cultures
are always inscribed into an order of cultural legitimacy that imposes upon
them an awareness of their own dependence. On the other hand, the relationship of domination, symbolic or not, is never symmetrical: "A dominant culture does not define itself in the first place by what it renounces,
whereas the dominated are always concerned with what the dominant refuses them, whatever is their attitude: resignation, denial, contestation,
imitation, or repression."[31]

To leave aside the implicit and the spontaneous linked with the concept of popular culture leads us back to our original question: how to articulate without simply alternating between these two models of popular culture that are, on one hand, a description of mechanisms that make the dominated internalize their own cultural illegitimacy, and on the other, a recognition of the manifestations by which a dominated culture "comes to organize in a symbolic coherence proper to it, experiences determined by its condition."[32] The answer is not easy, balanced between two perspectives: the first is to sort from among the most subjugated practices on one side and, on the other, those that ignore domination or negotiate with it; the second considers that each popular practice or discourse might be the object of two analyses, showing in turn its autonomy and its dependence. Such a road is narrow, difficult, and provisional, but it is today, I believe, the only one possible.

Notes

Chapter 1

1. I quote Vico's *Scienza Nuova* from the translation by Thomas Goddard Bergin and Max Harold Fish, *The New Science of Giambattista Vico: Unabridged Translation of the Third Edition (1744) with the addition of "Practice of the New Science"* (Ithaca, N.Y. and London: Cornell University Press, 1984).

2. On this tension see Gino Bedani, *Vico Revisited: Orthodoxy, Naturalism and Science in the* Scienza Nuova (Oxford, Hamburg, and Munich: Berg, 1989), 63–64.

3. On the tropological model of the *New Science* see Hayden White, "The Tropics of Discourse: The Deep Structure of the *New Science*," in *Giambattista Vico's Science of Humanity*, ed. Giorgio Tagliacozzo and Donald Philip Verene (Baltimore and London: Johns Hopkins University Press, 1976), 65–85.

4. I base my translations from Condorcet's *Esquisse* on *Outlines of an Historical View of the Progress of the Human Mind, Being a Posthumous Work of the Late M. de Condorcet* (Baltimore: Printed by G. Fryer for J. Frank, 1802).

5. This periodization is discussed by Keith Michael Baker in *Condorcet: From Natural Philosophy to Social Mathematics* (Chicago and London: University of Chicago Press, 1975), 360–61.

6. See Carla Hesse, "Enlightenment Epistemology and the Laws of Authorship in Revolutionary France, 1777–1793," *Representations* 30 (Spring 1990): 109–37, particularly 115–17.

7. *Les "Remontrances" de Malesherbes 1771–1775*, ed. Elisabeth Badinter (Paris: Union Générale d'Éditions, 1978).

8. *Discours prononcé à l'Académie française le jeudi 16 février 1775 à la réception de M. de Lamoignon de Malesherbes* (Paris, 1775).

9. Walter Ong, *Rhetoric, Romance, and Technology: Studies in the Interaction of Expression and Culture* (Ithaca, N.Y. and London: Cornell University Press, 1971), and *Orality and Literacy: The Technologizing of the Word* (London and New York: Methuen, 1982).

10. Jack Goody, *The Domestication of the Savage Mind* (Cambridge: Cambridge University Press, 1977).

11. Henri-Jean Martin, with Bruno Delmas, *Histoire et pouvoirs de l'écrit* (Paris, Librairie Académique Perrin, 1988), available in English as *The History and Power of Writing*, trans. Lydia G. Cochrane (Chicago and London: University of Chicago Press, 1994).

12. Henri-Jean Martin, "Le message écrit: l'émission," *Revue des Sciences Morales et Politiques, Travaux de l'Académie des Sciences Morales et Religieuses* 2 (1993): 229–38.

13. I am, of course, thinking of Lucien Febvre and Henri-Jean Martin's pioneering work, *L'Apparition du livre* (Paris: Albin Michel, 1958), available in English as *The Coming of the Book: The Impact of Printing, 1450–1800*, trans. David Gerard (London: Verso, 1984), and of Elizabeth Eisenstein's *The Printing Revolution in Early Modern Europe* (Cambridge: Cambridge University Press, 1983). The latter is an abridged version of *The Printing Press as an Agent of Change: Communications and Cultural Transformations in Early Modern Europe* (Cambridge: Cambridge University Press, 1979).

14. Paul Saenger and M. Heinlen, "Incunable Description and Its Implication for the Analysis of Fifteenth-Century Reading Habits," in *Printing the Written Word: The Social History of Books, circa 1450–1520*, ed Sandra Hindman (Ithaca, N.Y.: Cornell University Press, 1991), 225–58; and Margaret M. Smith, "Patterns of Incomplete Rubrication in Incunables and What They Suggest About Working Methods," in *Medieval Book Production: Assessing the Evidence*, ed. Linda L. Brownrigg (Los Altos Hills, Calif.: Red Gull Press, 1990), 133–45.

15. Jean-Pierre Drège, Mitchik Ishigami-Iagolnitzer, and Monique Cohen, eds., *Le livre et l'imprimerie en Extrême-Orient et en Asie du Sud–Est* (Bordeaux: Société des Bibliophiles de Guyenne, 1986); Evelyn S. Rawski, "Economic and Social Foundations of Late Imperial China," in *Popular Culture in Late Imperial China*, ed. David Johnson, Andrew J. Nathan, and Evelyn S. Rawski (Berkeley: University of California Press, 1985), 3–33; Monique Cohen and Nathalie Monnet, eds., *Impressions de Chine* (Paris: Bibliothèque Nationale, 1992); Henry D. Smith, II, "The History of the Book in Edo and Paris," in *Edo and Paris: Urban Life and the State in the Early Modern Era*, ed. James L. McClain, John M. Merriman, and Ugawa Kaoru (Ithaca, N.Y. and London: Cornell University Press, 1979), 332–52.

16. Armando Petrucci, "Alle origine del libro moderno. Libri da banco, libri da bisaccia, libretti da mano," in *Libri, scrittura e pubblico nel Rinascimento: Guida storica e critica*, ed. A. Petrucci (Rome and Bari: Laterza, 1979), 137–56.

17. Paul Saenger, "Silent Reading: Its Impact on Late Medieval Script and Society," *Viator: Medieval and Renaissance Studies* 13 (1982): 367–414; "Physiologie de la lecture et séparation des mots," *Annales E. S. C.* (1989): 939–52; "The Separation of Words and the Order of Words: The Genesis of Medieval Reading," *Scrittura e Civiltà* 14 (1990): 49–74.

18. Bernard Knox, "Silent Reading in Antiquity," *Greek, Roman, and Byzantine Studies* 9 (1968): 421–35.

19. Jesper Svenbro, *Phrasikleia: Anthropologie de la lecture en Grèce ancienne* (Paris: Éditions La Découverte, 1988).

20. William V. Harris, *Ancient Literacy* (Cambridge, Mass.: Harvard University Press, 1989).

21. Margít Frenk, "Lectores y oidores: La difusión oral de la literatura en el Siglo de Oro," in *Actas del Septimo Congreso de la Asociación Internacional de Hispanistas*, ed. Giuseppe Bellini (Rome: Bulzoni, 1982), 1: 101–23.

22. F. Alessio, "Conservazione e modelli di sapere nel Medioevo," in *La memoria del sapere: Forme di conservazione e strutture organizzative dall'Antichità a oggi*, ed. Pietro Rossi (Rome and Bari: Laterza, 1988), 99–133.

23. Rolf Engelsing, "Die Perioden der Lesergeschichte in der Neuzeit: Das

statistische Ausmaß und die soziokulturelle Bedeutung der Lektüre," *Archiv für Geschichte des Buchwesens* 10 (1970): 945–1002. Cf. also the critical revisions of Erich Schön, *Der Verlust der Sinnlichkeit oder Die Verwandlungen des Lesers: Mentalitätswandel um 1800* (Stuttgart: Klett-Cotta, 1987); M. Nagl, "Wandlungen des Lesens in der Aufklärung: Plädoyer für einige Differenzierungen," in *Bibliotheken und Aufklärung*, ed. Werner Arnold and Peter Vodosek, Wolfenbutteler Schriften zur Geschichte des Buchwesens (Wiesbaden: Otto Harrassowitz, 1988), 14: 21–40; Reinhard Wittmann, *Geschichte des deutschen Buchhandels* (Munich: C. H. Beck, 1991).

24. Ann Blair, "Humanist Methods in Natural Philosophy: The Commonplace Book," *Journal of the History of Ideas* 53 (Oct–Dec 1992): 541–51.

25. Robert Darnton, "Readers Respond to Rousseau: The Fabrication of Romantic Sensitivity," in *The Great Cat Massacre and Other Episodes in French Cultural History* (New York: Basic Books, 1984), 215–56.

26. Geoffrey Nunberg, "The Places of Books in the Age of Electronic Reproduction," *Representations* 42 (Spring 1993): 13–37.

27. Cf. the observations in Alain Blanchard, ed., *Les débuts du codex* (Turnhout: Brepols, 1989), and two articles by Guglielmo Cavallo: "Testo, libro, lettura," in *Lo spazio letterario di Roma antica*, ed. Guglielmo Cavallo, Paolo Fedeli, and Andrea Giardina (Rome: Salerno editrice; vol. 2, "La circolazione del testo," 1989), 307–41, and "Libro e cultura scritta," in *Storia di Roma* (Turin: Einaudi; vol. 4, *Caratteri e morfologie*, 1989), 693–734.

28. L. Holtz, "Les mots latins désignant le livre au temps d'Augustin," in Blanchard, ed., *Les débuts du codex*, 105–13.

29. Armando Petrucci, "Il libro manoscritto," in *Letteratura italiana* (Turin: Einaudi; vol. 2, *Produzione e consumo*, 1983), 499–524.

30. *Marks in Books* (Cambridge, Mass.: Houghton Library, 1985). Two examples of analyses of manuscript notes in printed books are Lisa Jardine and Anthony Grafton, "'Studied for Action': How Gabriel Harvey Read His Livy," *Past & Present* 129 (Nov. 1990): 30–78, and Cathy Davidson, *Revolution and the Word: The Rise of the Novel in America* (New York: Oxford University Press, 1986), 75–79. An example of a reader in the time of the manuscript book is in R. Meyenberg and Gilbert Ouy, "Alain Chartier, lecteur d'Ovide," *Scrittura e Civiltà* 14 (1990): 75–103.

31. Mark Rose, *Authors and Owners: The Invention of Copyright* (Cambridge, Mass. and London: Harvard University Press, 1993), 58, which corrects Donald W. Nichol, "On the Use of 'Copy' and 'Copyright': A Scriblerian Coinage?" *The Library: The Transactions of the Bibliographical Society* (June 1990): 110–20.

32. Peter Jaszi, "On the Author Effect: Contemporary Copyright and Collective Creativity," *Cardozo Arts and Entertainment Law Journal* 10 (1992: "Intellectual Property and the Construction of Authorship"), 293–320; Annie Prassoloff, "Le droit d'auteur à l'âge de l'écrit concurrencé," *Textuel* 25 (1993: "Ecrire, voir, conter"), 119–29; and Jane C. Ginsburg, "Copyright Without Walls? Speculations on Literary Property in the Library of the Future," *Representations* 42 (Spring 1993): 53–73.

33. Roger Chartier, "Bibliothèques sans murs," in *L'ordre des livres: Lecteurs, auteurs, bibliothèques en Europe entre XIVe et XVIIIe siècle* (Aix-en-Provence: Alinéa, 1992), 69–94; available in English as "Libraries Without Walls," in *The Order of*

Books: Readers, Authors, and Libraries in Europe between the Fourteenth and Eighteenth Centuries, trans. Lydia G. Cochrane (Stanford, Calif.: Stanford University Press, 1994), 61–88; Jean Marie Goulemot, "En guise de conclusion: les bibliothèques imaginaires (fictions romanesques et utopies)," in *Histoire des bibliothèques françaises* (Paris: Promodis-Éditions du Cercle de la Librairie; vol. 2, "Les bibliothèques sous l'Ancien Régime," ed. Claude Jolly, 1989), 500–11.

34. Luciano Canfora, *La biblioteca scomparsa* (Palermo: Sellerio editore, 1986); *Alexandrie IIIe siècle av. J. C.: Tous les savoirs du monde ou le rêve d'universalité des Ptolémées*, ed. Christian Jacob and François de Polignac (Paris: Éditions Autrement, 1992).

35. Jay D. Bolter, *Writing Space: The Computer Hypertext, and the History of Writing* (Hillsdale, N.J.: L. Erlbaum, 1991).

36. Jorge L. Borges, "La biblioteca de Babel"; ("The Library of Babel," in Borges, *Labyrinths: Selected Stories and Other Writings*, ed. Donald A. Yates and James E. Irby (New York: New Directions, 1964), 54–55.

37. Donald F. McKenzie, *Bibliography and the Sociology of Texts,* The Panizzi Lectures 1985 (London: British Library, 1986).

38. Francisco Rico, "La *princeps* del *Lazarillo*: Título, capitulación y epígrafes de un texto apócrifo," in *Problemas del Lazarillo* (Madrid: Cátedra, 1988), 113–51.

39. Donald F. McKenzie, "Typography and Meaning: The Case of William Congreve," in *Buch und Buchhandel in Europa im achtzehnten Jahrhundert, / The Book and the Book Trade in Eighteenth Century Europe*, proceedings of the fifth D. Wolfenbüttel symposium, 1–3 November 1977, ed. Giles Barber and Bernhard Fabian (Hamburg: Hauswedell, 1981), 81–126.

40. Ernst R. Curtius, *Europaische Literatur und Lateinisches Mittelalter* (Bern: A. Francke AG Verlag, 1948), chap. 16; Hans Blumenberg, *Die Lesbarkeit der Welt* (Frankfurt: Suhrkamp, 1981).

41. Harold Love, *Scribal Publication in Seventeenth-Century England* (Oxford: Oxford University Press, 1993); *De bonne main: La communication manuscrite au XVIIIe siècle*, ed. François Moureau (Paris: Universitas; Oxford: Voltaire Foundation, 1993).

42. Louis-Sebastien Mercier, *L'An 2440: Rêve s'il en fut jamais* (1771; Bordeaux: Éditions Ducros, 1971, "La bibliothèque du roi"), 247–71.

Chapter 2

1. *The Tempest,* quoted from *The Illustrated Stratford Shakespeare* (London: Chancellor Press, 1982), 9–29. References are to act, scene, and line.

2. See the commentary of Louis Marin, "Le portrait du poète en roi: William Shakespeare, *La Tempête*, acte I, scènes 1 et 2 (1611)," in *Des pouvoirs de l'image: Gloses* (Paris: Éditions du Seuil, 1993), 169–85.

3. For a "Rosicrucian" interpretation of *The Tempest*, see Frances A. Yates, *Shakespeare's Last Plays: A New Approach* (London: Routledge and Kegan Paul, 1975).

4. Simone Balayé, *La Bibliothèque Nationale des origines à 1800* (Geneva: Li-

brairie Droz, 1988), 64; on the king's *Cabinet des livres* in the Louvre, see 156–57, n. 30.

    5. Ibid., 27.

    6. Ibid., 42.

    7. Ibid., 47, n. 196.

    8. Gabriel Naudé, *Advis pour dresser une bibliothèque*, reproduction of the 1644 edition, preceded by Claude Jolly, "*L'Advis*, manifeste de la bibliothèque érudite" (Paris: Aux Amateurs de Livres, 1990), 12–14.

    9. William H. Sherman, "'A Living Library': The Reading and Writings of John Dee," Ph.D. thesis, Cambridge University, 1991.

    10. Antoine Coron, "'Ut prosint aliis': Jacques-Auguste de Thou et sa bibliothèque," *Histoire des bibliothèques françaises*, 4 vols. (Paris: Promodis-Éditions du Cercle de la Librairie, 1988), vol. 2, *Les bibliothèques sous l'Ancien Régime 1530–1789*, ed. Claude Jolly, 100–125.

    11. Fernando J. Bouza Álvarez, *Del Escribano a la Biblioteca: La Civilización escrita europea en la alta edad moderna (Siglos XV–XVIII)* (Madrid: Editorial Sintesis, 1992), 131.

    12. Balayé, *La Bibliothèque Nationale*, 198–200.

    13. For a comparison of depictions of the donation of a church and of the dedication of a book, see the catalog for the exposition "Les Fastes du Gothique: Le siècle de Charles V," Galeries nationales du Grand Palais, 9 October 1981–1 February 1982 (Paris: Éditions de la Réunion des Musées Nationaux, 1981), in particular no. 53, "Jean Tissendier en donateur" (a statue of Jean Tissendier, bishop of Rieux, offering to God the ambulatory chapel ("de Rieux") constructed at his expense in the chevet of the church of the Cordeliers in Toulouse); no. 257, "Dominicus Grima *Lectura in Genesim*" (a miniature representing Dominique Grima presenting his work to Pope John XXII); and no. 285, "Bible historiale de Vaudetar" (a miniature showing Charles V receiving the Bible offered to him by his counselor Jean de Vaudetar). See also Georges Duby, *Fondements d'un nouvel humanisme 1280–1440* (Geneva: Éditions d'Art Albert Skira, 1966), "Le donateur et sa marque," 21–29.

    14. Cynthia J. Brown, "Text, Image, and Authorial Self-Consciousness in Late Medieval Paris," in *Printing the Written Word: The Social History of Books, circa 1450–1520*, ed. Sandra Hindman (Ithaca, N.Y. and London: Cornell University Press, 1991), 103–42, quotation 142.

    15. Michel Foucault, "Qu'est-ce qu'un auteur?" *Bulletin de la Société Française de Philosophie* 64 (July–September 1969): 73–104, available in English as "What Is an Author?" in *Textual Strategies: Perspectives in Post-Structural Criticism*, ed. Josué V. Harari (Ithaca, N.Y.: Cornell University Press, 1979), 141–60. For a historical reading of this text see Roger Chartier, "Figures of the Author," in his *The Order of Books: Readers, Authors, and Libraries in Europe Between the Fourteenth and Eighteenth Centuries*, trans. Lydia G. Cochrane (Cambridge: Polity Press; Stanford, Calif.: Stanford University Press, 1994), 25–60.

    16. Brown, "Text, Image, and Authorial Self-Consciousness," 104.

    17. Ruth Mortimer, *A Portrait of the Author in Sixteenth-Century France*, Hanes Foundation Lectures 1 (Chapel Hill: University of North Carolina Press, 1980).

18. Ibid., fig. 3.

19. Ibid., fig. 7.

20. Annie Parent[-Charon], "Ambroise Paré et ses imprimeurs-libraires," *Actes du colloque international "Ambroise Paré et son temps"*, Laval (Mayenne), 24–25 November 1990 (Laval: Association de commémoration du Quadricentenaire de la mort d'Ambroise Paré, 1990), 207–33.

21. Annie Parent[-Charon], *Les métiers du livre à Paris au XVIe siècle (1535–1560)* (Geneva: Droz, 1974), 98–121 and "Annexe: Quelques documents extraits du Minutier Central des notaires parisiens aux Archives Nationales," 286–311.

22. Ibid., 300–301.

23. Ibid., 301–2.

24. Jean Toulet, "Les reliures," in *Histoire de l'Édition française*, gen. eds. Henri-Jean Martin and Roger Chartier, 4 vols. (Paris: Promodis, 1982–6), vol. 1, *Le livre conquérant: Du Moyen Age au milieu du XVIIe siècle*, 530–39.

25. On the *Premier volume de la Bibliothèque de Sieur de La Croix du Maine*, see Claude Longeon, "Antoine Du Verdier et François de La Croix du Maine," in *Actes du Colloque Renaissance-Classicisme du Maine*, Le Mans, May 1971 (Paris: A.-G. Nizet, 1975), 213–33; Roger Chartier, "Libraries Without Walls," in his *The Order of Books*, 61–88.

26. Pascale Bourgain, "L'Édition des manuscrits," in Martin and Chartier, gen. eds., *Histoire de l'Édition française*, 1: 48–75, esp. 54.

27. Jean-François Marmontel, *Mémoires*, critical edition by John Renwick, 2 vols. (Clermont-Ferrand: G. de Bussac, 1972), 1: 212–17.

28. Roger Chartier, "L'Uomo di lettere," in *L'Uomo dell'Illuminismo*, ed. Michel Vovelle (Rome and Bari: Editori Laterza, 1992), 143–97, forthcoming in English translation (Chicago: University of Chicago Press).

29. Mary Beth Winn, "Antoine Vérard's Presentation Manuscripts and Printed Books," in *Manuscripts in the Fifty Years After the Invention of Printing: Some Papers Read at a Colloquium at the Warburg Institute on 12–13 March 1982*, ed. J. B. Trapp (London: Warburg Institute, University of London, 1983), 66–74.

30. Roméo Arbour, *Un éditeur d'oeuvres littéraires au XVIIe siècle: Toussaint Du Bray (1604–1636)* (Geneva: Droz, 1992), 108–16.

31. On Galileo's strategies in dedications see Mario Biagioli, *Galileo, Courtier: The Practice of Science in the Culture of Absolutism* (Chicago: University of Chicago Press, 1993).

32. Galileo Galilei, *Sidereus Nuncius/Le Messager Céleste*, trans. and ed. Isabelle Pantin (Paris: Les Belles Lettres, 1992), title page reproduced on page 1, quoted from *Sidereus Nuncius, or, The Sidereal Messenger*, trans. Albert Van Helden (Chicago: University of Chicago Press, 1989).

33. *Sidereus Nuncius / Le Messager Céleste*, 3; *Sidereus Nuncius, or, The Sidereal Messenger*, 31.

34. Isabelle Pantin, "La réception du *Sidereus Nuncius*," in Johannes Kepler, *Dissertatio cum Nuncio Sidereo / Discussion avec le Messager Céleste*, trans. and ed. Isabelle Pantin (Paris: Les Belles Lettres, 1993), ix–lxxvii.

35. Biagioli, *Galileo, Courtier*, chap. 11, "Discoveries and Etiquette," 103–57.

36. Roberto Zapperi, *Annibale Carraci: Ritratto di artista da giovane* (Turin:

Einaudi, 1989), available in French translation as *Annibale Carraci: Portrait de l'artiste en jeune homme* (Aix-en-Provence: Alinéa, 1990); Martin Warnke, *Hofkünster: Zur Vorgeschichte des modernen Künstlers* (Cologne: DuMont Buchverlag, 1985), available in English as *The Court Artist: On the Ancestry of the Modern Artist*, trans. David McLintock (Cambridge: Cambridge University Press, 1992).

37. Biagioli, *Galileo, Courtier*, chap. 5, "Courtly Comets," 267–311.

38. Ibid., 127–33, 151–53.

39. Corneille, *Oeuvres complètes*, ed. Georges Couton, 3 vols. (Paris: Gallimard, Bibliothèque de la Pléiade, 1980–7), 1:834, quoted from *Seven Plays of Corneille*, trans. Samuel Solomon (New York: Random House, 1969), 104. On the text, see Christian Jouhaud, "L'écrivain et le ministre: Corneille et Richelieu," *XVII Siècle* 182 (jan.–mars 1994): 135–42. For an overview of dedicatory epistles in seventeenth-century France, see Wolfgang Leiner, *Der Widmungsbrief in der französischen Literatur (1580–1715)* (Heidelberg: Carl Winter Verlag, 1965).

40. Chartier, *The Order of Books*, 77–80.

41. Fernando J. Bouza Álvarez, "La Biblioteca de El Escorial y el orden de los saberes en el siglo XVI," in *El Escorial: Arte, poder y cultura en la corte de Felipe II*, Universidad Complutense de Madrid, Cursos de Verano, El Escorial 1988 (Madrid, 1989), 81–99, quotation 88.

42. On Gesner see Alfredo Serrai, *Conrad Gesner*, ed. Maria Cochetti, which contains a bibliography of Gesner's works by Marco Menato (Rome: Bulzoni, 1990); Helmut Zedelmaier, *Bibliotheca Universalis und Bibliotheca Selecta: Das Problem der Ordnung des gelehrten Wissens in der frühen Neuzeit* (Cologne, Weimar, and Vienna: Böhlau Verlag, 1992).

43. Quoted in Jacqueline Cerquiglini-Toulet, *La couleur de la mélancolie: La fréquentation des livres au XIVe siècle 1300–1415* (Paris: Hatier, 1993), 160–61, and given here, adjusted, from *Froissart's Chronicles*, trans. and ed. John Jolliffe (New York: Modern Library, 1968), 362.

44. Paul Saenger, "Silent Reading and Its Impact on Late Medieval Script and Society," *Viator: Medieval and Renaissance Studies* 13 (1982)): 367–414, esp. 407–14.

45. William Nelson, "From 'Listen, Lordings' to 'Dear Reader'," *University of Toronto Quarterly: A Canadian Journal of the Humanities* 46, 2 (Winter 1976/7): 110–24.

46. Balayé, *La Bibliothèque Nationale*, 32.

47. François Rabelais, *Oeuvres complètes*, ed. Guy Demerson (Paris: Éditions du Seuil, l'Intégrale, 1973), 564–65, quoted from *The Five Books of Gargantua and Pantagruel*, trans. Jacques Le Clercq (New York: Random House/Modern Library, c1936), 492.

48. Ibid., 449; quoted from the *Five Books*, 372.

49. Quoted from Nelson, "From 'Listen, Lordings' to 'Dear Reader'," 114–15.

50. Lisa Jardine and Anthony Grafton, "'Studied for Action': How Gabriel Harvey Read His Livy," *Past and Present* 129 (Nov. 1990): 30–78, quotation 35.

51. On patronage and patrons in the sixteenth and seventeenth centuries, see Guy Fitch Lytle and Stephen Orgel, eds., *Patronage in the Renaissance* (Princeton, N.J.: Princeton University Press, 1981); Alain Viala, *Naissance de l'écrivain: Sociologie de la littérature à l'âge classique* (Paris: Éditions de Minuit, 1985) and the review of

that work by Christian Jouhaud, "Histoire et histoire littéraire: Naissance de l'écrivain," *Annales E.S.C.* (1988): 849–66; *L'Age d'or du mécénat (1598–1661)*, Actes du Colloque International CNRS, March 1983, "Le Mécénat en Europe, et particulièrement en France avant Colbert," ed. Roland Mousnier and Jean Mesnard for the Société d'Étude du XVIIe Siècle (Paris: Éditions du Centre National de la Recherche Scientifique, 1985).

52. Furetière, *Le Roman bourgeois*, ed. Jacques Prévot (Paris: Gallimard, Folio, 1981), 234–45.

Chapter 3

1. *Le Registre de La Grange (1659–1685)*, ed. Bert Edward Young and Grace Philputt Young, 2 vols. (Geneva: Droz, 1947), 1:99.

2. *Gazette*, 1668, 695–96.

3. Louis XIV, *Mémoires: Suivi de réflexions sur le métier de Roi: Instructions au duc d'Anjou: Projet de harangue*, ed. Jean Longnon (Paris: Tallandier, 1978), 267–77.

4. Molière, "Au Roy sur sa conqueste de la Franche-Comté," in *Oeuvres de Molière*, new ed., rev., ed. Eugène Despois and Paul Mesnard, 18 vols. (Paris: Hachette, 1881–1912), vol. 9 (1886), 584–85.

5. *Le Registre de La Grange*, 1: 101.

6. *Gazette*, 1668, 1182. Notices on the performances of the comedy can be found conveniently gathered in one place in Georges Mongrédien, *Recueil de textes et de documents du XVIIe siècle relatifs à Molière*, 2 vols. (Paris: Éditions du C.N.R.S., 1965, 1973).

7. See the exemplary works of Donald F. McKenzie, "Typography and Meaning: The Case of William Congreve," in *Buch und Buchhandel in Europa im achtzehnten Jahrhundert/The Book and the Book Trade in Eighteenth-Century Europe*, proceedings of the fifth Wolfenbüttel symposium, 1–3 November 1977, ed. Giles Barber and Bernhard Fabian (Hamburg: Hauswedell 1981), 81–126; McKenzie, *Bibliography and the Sociology of Texts*, The Panizzi Lectures 1985 (London: British Library, 1986).

8. The lack of critical interest in *George Dandin* can be measured by a glance at two bibliographies of works regarding Molière: Paul Frédéric Saintonge and Robert Wilson Christ, *Fifty Years of Molière Studies: A Bibliography, 1892–1951* (Baltimore: Johns Hopkins University Press; London: H. Milford, Oxford University Press, 1942), 196–97; and Saintonge, "Thirty Years of Molière Studies: A Bibliography, 1942–1971," in *Molière and the Commonwealth of Letters: Patrimony and Posterity*, ed. Roger Johnson, Jr., Editha S. Neumann, and Guy Trail (Jackson: University Press of Mississippi, 1975), 796–97.

9. Lionel Gossman, *Men and Masks: A Study of Molière* (Baltimore: Johns Hopkins University Press, 1963), 146–63.

10. On the first two productions, see Maurice Descotes, "Nouvelles interprétations moliéresques," *Oeuvres et critiques* 6, 1, *Visages de Molière* (1981): 35–55; R. Saint-Paul, "George Dandin de Molière à nos jours: Trois siècles de mise en scène en France," doctoral dissertation, Université de Paris, 1972, 85–109. For an example

of a critical study elicited by Planchon's 1958 staging of the play, see Joan Crow, "Reflections on George Dandin," in *Molière: Stage and Study; Essays in Honour of W. G. Moore*, ed. W. D. Howarth and Merlin Thomas (Oxford: Clarendon Press, 1973), 3–12.

11. Roger Planchon, "En préface," in *George Dandin ou le Mari Confondu*, program for the performances at the Théâtre National Populaire, Villeurbanne, 16 March–4 April 1987, 10–16.

12. Molière, *La Critique de l'École des Femmes*, in Molière, *Oeuvres complètes*, texts established, presented, and annotated by Georges Couton, 2 vols. (Paris: Gallimard/Bibliothèque de La Pléiade, 1971), vol. 1 (1971), 635–68, quotation 661, quoted from *Eight Plays by Molière*, trans. Morris Bishop (New York: Modern Library, 1957), 115.

13. *Relation de la Feste de Versailles du dix-huitième Juillet mil six cens soixante huit* (Paris: Le Petit, 1668), 60 pages; reprinted in André Félibien, *Les Fêtes de Versailles: Chroniques de 1668 et 1674*, texts presented by Martin Meade (Paris: Éditions Dédale, Maisonneuve et Larose, 1994), 31–93, quotation 45.

14. *Le Grand divertissement royal de Versailles* (Paris: Ballard, 1668), 20 pages; reprinted in *Oeuvres complètes* (La Pléiade), 2: 451–61.

15. *Lettre en vers à Madame*, 21 July 1668, 3–4.

16. See Albert Jean Guibert, *Bibliographie des oeuvres de Molière publiées au XVIIe siècle*, 2 vols. (Paris: Éditions du C.N.R.S., 1961), 1: 283–92.

17. Molière, *L'Amour médecin*, in *Oeuvres complètes* (La Pléiade), 2: 87–120, quotation, 95, quoted from *The Works of Mr. de Molière*, trans. John Ozell (London, 1714), reprint, 3 vols. (New York: Benjamin Blom, 1967), 3: 85.

18. The radical heterogeneity of the comedy and the "pastoral" is one of the commonplaces of critical comment on the 1668 *divertissement*. For one example, see W. D. Howarth, *Molière: A Playwright and His Audience* (Cambridge and New York: Cambridge University Press, 1982), 218–19, where Howarth states that there is "absolutely no integration between the play and its spectacular framework." Among the few exceptions to this rule are the readings of Friedrich Böttger, *Die "Comédie-Ballet" von Molière-Lully* (Berlin: Paul Funk, n.d. [1931], and F. L. Lawrence, *Molière: The Comedy of Unreason* (New Orleans: Tulane Studies in Romance Languages and Literature, 1968), 45–46. Lawrence states, "My conviction that *George Dandin* is a drama of courtly love seen through the reverse side of the glass was fostered and finds its ratification in the little pastoral which Molière wrote for the entr'actes of the main drama at the Versailles extravaganza where *George Dandin* was first performed." It should be noted, however, that the pastoral (which was by no means "little") was not written for the entr'actes of the comedy; rather, it was the pastoral that constituted the larger form into which the acts of the comedy were fitted.

19. Helen Purkis, "Les intermèdes musicaux de 'George Dandin,'" in *Baroque: La fête théâtrale et les sources de l'opéra*, Acts of the 4th session, Journées Internationales d'Étude du Baroque, Montauban 1970, 5e cahier, 1972, 63–69. See also the analysis of *Amphytrion* in Paul Bénichou, *Morales du grand siècle* (Paris: Gallimard, 1948; reprint, Idées, 1983), 267–75; available in English as *Man and Ethics: Studies in French Classicism*, trans. Elizabeth Hughes (Garden City, N.Y.: Anchor Books, 1971).

20. For a comparison of the vocabulary of Molière, Racine, and Corneille, see Charles Louis Livet, *Lexique de la langue de Molière comparée à celle des écrivains de son temps* (Paris: Imprimerie Nationale, 1895–7); Bryant C. Freeman and Alan Batson, *Concordance du théâtre et des poésies de Jean Racine*, 2 vols. (Ithaca, N.Y.: Cornell University Press, 1968); Charles Muller, *Etude de statistique lexicale: Le vocabulaire du théâtre de Pierre Corneille* (Paris: Larousse, 1967).

21. *Relation de la Feste de Versailles du dix-huitième Juillet mil six cens soixante huit*.

22. Guibert, *Bibliographie des oeuvres de Molière*, 1:508–12 and 2:23–24.

23. The fête of 18 July and that of 17 September (which featured, according to the *Gazette*, a supper served in the Ménagerie; the illumination of the Fer-à-Cheval, the château, and the grotto; and a fireworks display) together cost 117,033 livres, 2 sous, 9 deniers, according to the *Comptes des Bâtiments du Roi sous le règne de Louis XIV*, ed. Jules Marie Joseph Guiffrey, 5 vols. (Paris: Imprimerie Nationale, 1881–1901), vol. 1, *Colbert 1664–1680* (1881), 302–8. The bill, divided into ninety-one headings, attests that 65 percent of the expense was for the materials, decorations, and ornaments for the *fabriques* (constructions); 16.5 percent for the wages of the workers employed to put them up (and take them down afterward); and 15 percent for the illuminations and the fireworks. The account mentions the presence of a large contingent of Swiss Guards, who "served 3,440 days during the two fetes at Versailles, at 20 sous per day," and it gives the names of the artists pressed into service for the decoration of the festive hall and the ballroom (the painter Louis Le Hongre, and the sculptors Jacques Houzeau, Étienne Le Hongre, Gérard Van Obstal, and Louis Lerambert).

24. See Bernard Teyssèdre, *L'art au siècle de Louis XIV* (Paris: Livre de poche, 1967), 140–45; Jacques Vanuxem, "La scénographie des fêtes de Louis XIV auxquelles Molière a participé," *XVIIe Siècle* 98–99 (1973): 77–90; Jean-Marie Apostolidès, *Le Roi-machine: Spectacle et politique au temps de Louis XIV* (Paris: Éditions de Minuit, 1981), 86–92.

25. Richard Alewyn, *Aus der Welt des Barock* (Stuttgart: J. B. Metzler, 1957), available in French translation as *L'univers du baroque* (Paris: Gonthier, 1964).

26. On the aristocratic idealization of the chivalric and rustic noble life, see Norbert Elias, *The Court Society*, trans. Edmund Jephcott (Oxford: Blackwell, 1983), 214–67.

27. On the island motif in Versailles festivities, see Oreste Ranum, "Islands and the Self in a Ludovician Fête," in *Sun King: The Ascendancy of French Culture During the Reign of Louis XIV*, papers from a symposium sponsored by the Folger Institute, March 1985, ed. David Lee Rubin (Washington, D.C.: Folger Shakespeare Library; London: Associated University Presses, 1992), 17–34. Ranum notes, "The transcendent moment of the 1668 fête carried the same message as that of the Enchanted Isle of 1664, but the entire château had momentarily become an island palace, residence of the gods under Apollo's attentive and fertile gaze," p. 28.

28. Teyssèdre, *L'Art au siècle de Louis XIV*, 76; 134–40; 81–82.

29. The décor is not the one engraved by Lepautre for the 1679 edition of the *Relation*, which shows instead the scenery for the last interlude, the combat and reconciliation of the followers of Bacchus and of Love.

30. Abbé de Montigny, *La Fête de Versailles du 18 juillet 1668*, Bibliothèque de l'Arsenal, MS 5418, Recueil Conrart in-folio, vol. 9, 1109–19; printed text in *Recueil de diverses pièces faites par plusieurs personnes* (The Hague: J. and D. Stencker, 1669).

31. *Lettre en vers à Madame*, 21 July 1668, 3–4.

32. Christiaan Huygens, *Oeuvres complètes*, 22 vols. (The Hague: M. Nijhoff, 1888–1950), vol. 6, *Correspondance 1666–1669*, letter of 27 July to Philippe Doublet, 245–46. According to the *Comptes des Bâtiments du Roi*, Huygens received 6,000 livres in December 1668 "for his appointments during the present year."

33. Bénichou, *Morales du grand siècle*; Erich Auerbach, *Mimesis: The Representation of Reality in Western Literature*, trans. Willard R. Trask (Princeton, N.J.: Princeton University Press, 1953).

34. *Lettre en vers à Madame*, 10 November 1668, 2.

35. Molière, *George Dandin ou le Mari Confondu*, in *Oeuvres complètes* (La Pléiade), 2: 463–503, quotation 465–66, quoted from Molière, *Don Juan and Other Plays*, trans. George Graveley and Ian Maclean, ed. Ian Maclean (Oxford and New York: Oxford University Press, 1989), 137.

36. This interpretation of the doubling of Dandin can be found in Danilo Romano, *Essai sur le comique de Molière* (Berne: A. Francke, 1950); Jules Brody, "Esthétique et société chez Molière," in *Dramaturgie et société: Rapports entre l'oeuvre théâtrale, son interpretation et son public aux XVIe et XVIIe siècles*, Nancy, 14–21 April 1967, 2 vols. (Paris: Éditions du C.N.R.S., 1968), 1: 307–26.

37. Gossman, *Men and Masks*, 161–62: "Dandin's whole behavior is marked by this dual attitude of love and hate, of self-love and self-hate. He must inevitably seek to be humiliated by his idols in order that their divinity be upheld, and he must inevitably resent this divinity because it is the obstacle to his own. . . . The George Dandin who comments is the resentful George — it is he who seeks to 'désabuser le père et la mère' — and the George who is commented on is the idolatrous George."

38. Harold C. Knutson, *Molière: An Archetypal Approach* (Toronto and Buffalo: University of Toronto Press, 1976), 154: "That belated wisdom cohabits in Dandin with the memory of folly explains the distinctive *dédoublement* of this main character and the constant dialogue that goes on within him."

39. Ralph Albanese, Jr., "Solipsisme et parole dans *George Dandin*," *Kentucky Romance Quarterly* 27 (1980): 421–34.

40. Molière, *La Critique de l'École des Femmes* (La Pléiade), 1: 659, quoted from *Eight Plays by Molière*, 113–14.

41. Madeleine Jurgens and Elizabeth Maxfield-Miller, *Cent ans de recherches sur Molière, sur sa famille et sur les comédiens de sa troupe* (Paris: SEVPEN, 1963), 554–84; description of the costume for the role of Dandin, p. 567. See also the comments of Stephen Varick Dock, *Costume and Fashion in the Plays of Jean-Baptiste Poquelin Molière: A Seventeenth-Century Perspective* (Geneva: Slatkine, 1992), 203–8.

42. François Rabelais, *Le Tiers-Livre*, Chapter 41, in Rabelais, *Oeuvres complètes* (Paris: Éditions du Seuil/L'Intégrale, 1973), 518–21, quoted here from *The Complete Works of François Rabelais*, trans. Donald M. Frame (Berkeley, Los Angeles, and Oxford: University of California Press, 1991), 380–81. The term *dendins* is one of the insults that the bakers of Lerné hurl at the shepherds who are Gargantua's subjects: *Gargantua*, in *Oeuvres complètes*, 119.

43. See Nathan Gross, *From Gesture to Idea — Esthetics and Ethics in Molière's Comedy* (New York: Columbia University Press, 1982), 127–38. For Gross, *George Dandin* "takes the form of a series of trials" (127).

44. See the concordant conclusions of Jean-Marie Constant, *Nobles et paysans in Beauce aux XVIe et XVIIe siècles* (Lille: Service de Reproduction des Thèses, Université de Lille III, 1981), Chapters 3 and 4; James B. Wood, *The Nobility of the Election of Bayeux, 1463–1666: Continuity Through Change* (Princeton, N.J.: Princeton University Press, 1980).

45. Constant, *Nobles et paysans*, 70–73, at the paragraph, "Des paysans ont-il pu s'anoblir avant 1560?"

46. Constant, *Nobles et paysans*, agrees on this point (p. 233). Constant estimates at 15.3 percent of nobles in the Beauce married into families of commoners, officials, and bourgeois for the period 1660–1700, as opposed to 1.3 percent for the period 1600–1660. Jean Jacquart, *La Crise rurale en Ile-de-France, 1550–1670* (Paris: A. Colin, 1974), 534, concurs.

47. Madame de Sévigné, *Correspondance*, ed. Roger Duchêne, 3 vols. (Paris: Gallimard/La Pléiade, 1972–78), vol. 1, *Mars 1646–juillet 1675* (1972), 99–102.

48. For two examples of research into the situation in the French provinces, see Wood, *The Nobility of the Election of Bayeux*, Chapter 1, and Jean Meyer, *La noblesse bretonne au XVIIIe siècle*, 2 vols. (Paris: SEVPEN, 1966), 1: 29–61. In the Bayeux election, 6 percent of nobles who were verified were put back under the *taille*; in Brittany, the percentage seems to have been much higher.

49. Pierre Jean Grosley, "Recherches sur la noblesse utérine de Champagne," in Grosley, *Recherches pour servir à l'histoire du droit français* (Paris: Veuve Estienne & fils, 1752), 183–250, which cites the customs of Troyes, Châlons, Meaux, Vitry, Chaumont, and Sens.

50. Jean de La Bruyère, *Les Caractères de Théophraste traduits du grec; avec les Caractères ou les Moeurs de ce siècle*, ed. Robert Garapon (Paris: Garnier, 1962), 11, "De quelques usages," 416.

51. Madame de Sévigné, *Correspondance*, letter to Bussy Rabutin of 4 December 1668, 105–6.

52. James F. Gaines, *Social Structures in Molière's Theater* (Columbus: Ohio University Press, 1984), 148–55.

Chapter 4

1. Claude Grignon and Jean-Claude Passeron, *Le Savant et le populaire: misérabilisme et populisme en sociologie et en littérature* (Paris: Gallimard/Le Seuil, Hautes Études, 1989), 36.

2. Ibid., 37.

3. Robert Muchembled, *Culture populaire et culture des élites dans la France moderne (XVe–XVIIIe siècles)* (Paris: Flammarion, 1978), 341. Translated by Lydia G. Cochrane as *Popular Culture and Elite Culture in France, 1400–1750* (Baton Rouge: Louisiana State University Press, 1985). In the preface to a new edition of

his book (Paris: Flammarion, 1991) the author presents some important nuances to his point of view.

4. Peter Burke, *Popular Culture in Early Modern Europe* (New York: Harper and Row, 1978), 207, 208, 270.

5. Jacques Le Goff, "Ecclesiastical Culture and Folklore in the Middle Ages: Saint Marcellus of Paris and the Dragon," in *Time, Work, and Culture in the Middle Ages*, trans. Arthur Goldhammer (Chicago: University of Chicago Press, 1980), 159–88, quotation on 185. Originally published as "Culture ecclésiastique et culture folklorique au Moyen Âge: Saint Marcel de Paris et le dragon," in *Pour une autre Moyen Âge: Temps, travail et culture en Occident: 18 essais* (Paris: Gallimard, 1977), 236–79, quotation on p. 276.

6. Jean-Claude Schmitt, "'Religion populaire' et culture folklorique," *Annales E.S.C.* (1976): 941–53.

7. Eugen Weber, *Peasants into Frenchmen: The Modernization of Rural France, 1870–1914* (Stanford, Calif.: Stanford University Press, 1976).

8. Lawrence W. Levine, *Highbrow/Lowbrow: The Emergence of Cultural Hierarchy in America* (Cambridge, Mass.: Harvard University Press, 1988), 208–9.

9. David D. Hall, review of Levine, *Highbrow/Lowbrow*, *Reviews in American History* (March 1990): 10–14.

10. Pierre Bourdieu, *Les règles de l'art: Genèse et structure du champ littéraire* (Paris: Éditions du Seuil, 1992), 80. See also in English "The Field of Cultural Production, or the Economic World Reversed," in Pierre Bourdieu, *The Field of Cultural Production: Essays on Art and Literature*, edited and introduced by Randall Johnson (New York: Columbia University Press, 1993), 29–73.

11. Michel Foucault, "The Discourse on Language," in *The Archeology of Knowledge* (New York: Pantheon, 1972), 229. Originally published as *L'ordre du discours* (Paris: Gallimard, 1971), 54.

12. Paul Ricoeur, *Du texte à l'action: Essais d'herméneutique II* (Paris: Éditions du Seuil, 1986), 152–53. Translated by Kathleen Blamey and John B. Thompson as *From Text to Action* (Evanston, Ill.: Northwestern University Press, 1991).

13. Michel de Certeau, *The Practice of Everyday Life*, trans. Steven Rendall (Berkeley: University of California Press, 1984), xii–xiii. Originally published as *L'invention du quotidien: 1. Arts de faire* (Paris: Gallimard, 1990 [1980]), xxxvii.

14. Ibid., xxi. In original, xlix.

15. Richard Hoggart, *The Uses of Literacy: Aspects of Working-Class Life with Special Reference to Publications and Entertainments* (London: Chatto and Windus, 1957). See also the French translation and the introduction by Jean-Claude Passeron: *La culture du pauvre: Etude sur le style de vie des classes populaires en Angleterre* (Paris: Éditions de Minuit, 1970).

16. Janice A. Radway, *Reading the Romance: Women, Patriarchy, and Popular Literature* (Chapel Hill: University of North Carolina Press, 1984), 221–22.

17. Ibid., 17.

18. Roger Chartier, "Des 'secrétaires' pour le peuple? Les modèles epistolaires de l'Ancien Régime entre littérature de cour et livre de colportage," in *La Correspondance: Les usages de la lettre au XIXe siècle*, ed. Chartier (Paris: Fayard, 1991), 159–207.

19. Roger Chartier, "The Literature of Roguery in the *Bibliothèque bleue*," in Chartier, *The Cultural Uses of Print in Early Modern France* (Princeton, N.J.: Princeton University Press, 1987), 265–342. Originally published as "Figures littéraires et expériences sociales: la littérature de la gueuserie dans la Bibliothèque bleue," in Chartier, *Lectures et lecteurs dans la France d'Ancien Régime* (Paris: Éditions du Seuil, 1987), 271–351.

20. Martyn Lyons and Lucy Taksa, *Australian Readers Remember: An Oral History of Reading, 1890–1930* (Melbourne: Oxford University Press, 1992).

21. Fritz Nies, *Bahn und Bett und Blutenduft: Eine Reise durch die Welt der Leserbilder* (Darmstadt: Wissenschaftliche Buchgesellschaft, 1991).

22. Tessa Watt, *Cheap Print and Popular Piety, 1550–1640* (Cambridge: Cambridge University Press, 1991).

23. Jean Hébrard, "Comment Valentin Jamerey-Duval apprit-il à lire? L'autodidaxie exemplaire," in *Pratiques de la lecture*, ed. Roger Chartier (Marseilles: Rivages, 1985), 23–60; and "Les nouveaux lecteurs," in *Histoire de L'Edition française*, ed. Roger Chartier and Henri-Jean Martin, vol. III, *Le temps des éditeurs: Du romantisme à la Belle Epoque* (Paris: Fayard/Cercle de la Libraire, 1990 [1985]), 526–65.

24. David D. Hall, *Worlds of Wonder, Days of Judgment: Popular Religious Belief in Early New England* (Cambridge, Mass.: Harvard University Press, 1989), 39–43; Marie-Elisabeth Ducreux, "Readers unto Death: Books and Readers in Eighteenth-Century Bohemia," in *The Culture of Print: Power and the Uses of Print in Early Modern Europe*, ed. Roger Chartier (Princeton, N.J.: Princeton University Press, 1989), 191–229, originally published as "Lire à en mourir: Livres et lecteurs en Bohème au XVIIIe siècle," in *Les usages de l'imprimé (XVe–XIXe siècle)*, ed. Roger Chartier (Paris: Fayard, 1987), 283–303; Sarah T. Nalle, "Literacy and Culture in Early Modern Castile," *Past and Present* 125 (November 1989), 65–96.

25. Catherine Velay Vallantin, *L'Histoire des contes* (Paris: Fayard, 1992).

26. Carlo Ginzburg, *The Cheese and the Worms: The Cosmos of a Sixteenth-Century Miller*, trans. John Tedeschi and Anne Tedeschi (Baltimore: Johns Hopkins University Press, 1980). Originally published as *Il formaggio e i vermi: Il cosmo di un mugnaio del'500* (Turin: Einaudi, 1970).

27. Lisa Jardine and Anthony Grafton, "'Studied for Action': How Gabriel Harvey Read His Livy," *Past and Present* 129 (November 1990), 30–78; Ann Blair, "Humanist Methods in Natural Philosophy: The Commonplace Book," *Journal of the History of Ideas* 53 (Oct–Dec 1992): 541–51.

28. John E. Toews, "Intellectual History after the Linguistic Turn: The Autonomy of Meaning and the Irreducibility of Experience," *American Historical Review* 92 (October 1987): 879–907, quotation 882. For the two poles of the discussion, see David Harlan, "Intellectual History and the Return of Literature," *American Historical Review* 94 (June 1989): 581–609, and Gabrielle M. Spiegel, "History, Historicism, and the Social Logic of the Text in the Middle Ages," *Speculum: A Journal of Medieval Studies* 65 (January 1990): 59–86.

29. Pierre Bourdieu, *Choses dites* (Paris: Éditions de Minuit, 1987), 76, 137. Translated by Matthew Adamson as *In Other Words: Essays Towards a Reflexive Sociology* (Stanford, Calif.: Stanford University Press, 1990).

30. Giovanni Levi, "Les usages de la biographie," *Annales E.S.C.* (1989):

1325–35, (quotation 1333), discusses the definition of the concept of representation proposed in Roger Chartier, "Le monde comme représentation," *Annales E.S.C.* (1989): 1505–20.

31. Passeron, *Le Savant et le populaire*, 61.

32. Ibid., 92.

Select Bibliography

Alewyn, Richard. *L'Univers du Baroque*. Paris: Éditions Gonthier, 1964.

———. *Das grosse Welttheater: Die Epoche der hofischen Feste*. Second edition. Munich: C. H. Beck, 1985.

———. *Deutsche Barockforschung*. Cologne: Kiepenheuer und Wiltsch, 1965.

Apostolidès, Jean-Marie. *Le Roi-machine: Spectacle et politique au temps de Louis XIV*. Paris: Éditions de Minuit, 1964.

Auerbach, Erich. *Mimesis: The Representation of Reality in Western Literature*. Translated by Willard R. Trask. Princeton, N.J.: Princeton University Press, 1953.

———. *Scenes from the Drama of European Literature*. Translated by Ralph Manheim. Minneapolis: University of Minnesota Press, 1984.

Balayé, Simone. *La Bibliothèque Nationale des origines à 1800*. Geneva: Librairie Droz, 1988.

Bäuml, Franz H. "Varieties and Consequences of Medieval Literacy and Illiteracy." *Speculum* 55 (1974): 237–65.

Bénichou, Paul. *Man and Ethics: Studies in French Classicism*. Translated by Elizabeth Hughes. Garden City, N.Y.: Anchor Books, 1971.

Biagioli, Mario. *Galileo, Courtier: The Practice of Science in the Culture of Absolutism*. Chicago: University of Chicago Press, 1993.

Blair, Ann. "Humanist Methods in Natural Philosophy: The Commonplace Book." *Journal of the History of Ideas* 53 (Oct–Dec 1992): 541–51.

Blanchard, Alain, ed. *Les Débuts du codex*. Turnhout: Brepols, 1989.

Blumenberg, Hans. *Die Lesbarkeit der Welt*. Frankfurt: Suhrkamp, 1981.

Bolter, Jay D. *Writing Space: The Computer, Hypertext, and the History of Writing*. Hillsdale, N.J.: L. Erlbaum, 1991.

Bourdieu, Pierre. *Les règles de l'art: Genèse et structure du champ littéraire*. Paris: Éditions du Seuil, 1992.

———. *The Field of Cultural Production: Essays on Art and Literature*. Edited and introduced by Randall Johnson. New York: Columbia University Press, 1993.

Bouza Álvarez, Fernando J. *Del Escribano a la Biblioteca: La Civilización escrita europea en la alta edad moderna (Siglos XV–XVII)*. Madrid: Editorial Síntesis, 1992.

Boyarin, Jonathan, ed. *The Ethnography of Reading*. Berkeley: University of California Press, 1992.

Braida, Lodovica. *Le Guide del tempo: Produzione, contenuti e forme degli almanacchi piemontesi nel Settecento*. Turin: Deputazione Subalpina di Storia Patria, 1989.

Brennan, Michael. *Literary Patronage in the English Renaissance: The Pembroke Family*. London and New York: Routledge, 1988.

Brown, Cedric C., ed. *Patronage, Politics, and Literary Traditions in England, 1558–1658*. Detroit: Wayne State University Press, 1993.

Brownrigg, Linda L., ed. *Medieval Book Production: Assessing the Evidence*. Los Altos Hills, Calif.: Red Gull Press, 1990.

Burke, Peter. *Popular Culture in Early Modern Europe*. New York: Harper and Row, 1978.

Canfora, Luciano. "Lire à Athènes et à Rome." *Annales E.S.C.* (1989): 925–37.

Cavallo, Guglielmo. "Libro a cultura scritta." In *Storia di Roma*, ed. Arnaldo Momigliano and Aldo Schiavone, vol. 4, *Caratteri e morfologie*, 693–734. Turin: Einaudi, 1989.

———. "Testo, libro, lettura. In *Lo spazio letterario di Roma antica*, ed. Guglielmo Cavallo, Paolo Fedeli, and Andrea Giardina, vol. 2, *La circolazione del testo*, 307–41. Rome: Salerno Editrice, 1989.

Cerquiglini-Toulet, Jacqueline. *La couleur de la mélancolie: La fréquentation des livres au XIVe siècle 1300–1415*. Paris: Hatier, 1993.

Certeau, Michel de. *The Practice of Everyday Life*. Translated by Steven F. Rendall. Berkeley: University of California Press, 1984.

Chartier, Roger. *The Order of Books: Readers, Authors, and Libraries in Europe Between the Fourteenth and Eighteenth Centuries*. Translated by Lydia G. Cochrane. Stanford, Calif.: Stanford University Press, 1994.

———. "L'Uomo di lettere." In *L'Uomo dell'Illuminismo*, ed. Michel Vovelle, 143–97. Rome and Bari: Editori Laterza, 1992.

———. "Trajectoires et tensions culturelles sous l'Ancien Régime." In *Histoire de la France*, ed. André Burgière and Jacques Revel, vol. 4, *Les formes de la culture*, 307–92. Paris: Éditions du Seuil, 1993.

———, ed. *The Culture of Print: Power and the Uses of Print in Early Modern Europe*. Translated by Lydia G. Cochrane. Princeton, N.J.: Princeton University Press, 1989.

———, ed. *La correspondance: Les usages de la lettre au XIXe siècle*. Paris: Fayard, 1991.

Clanchy, M. T. *From Memory to Written Record: England, 1066–1307*. Cambridge, Mass.: Harvard University Press, 1979.

Curtius, Ernst Robert. *European Literature and the Latin Middle Ages*. Translated by Willard R. Trask. Princeton, N.J.: Princeton University Press, 1973.

Darnton, Robert. *The Kiss of Lamourette: Reflections in Cultural History*. New York: Norton, 1990.

———. *Gens de lettres et gens du livre*. Paris: Éditions Odile Jacob, 1992.

Davidson, Cathy. *Revolution and the Word: The Rise of the Novel in America*. New York: Oxford University Press, 1986.

Davis, Natalie Zemon. *Society and Culture in Early Modern France*. Stanford, Calif.: Stanford University Press, 1975.

———. "Toward Mixtures and Margins." *American Historical Review* 97, 5 (December 1992): 1409–16.

Détienne, Marcel, ed. *Les Savoirs de l'écriture: en Grèce ancienne*. Lille: Presses Universitaires de Lille, 1992.

Eisenstein, Elizabeth. *The Printing Press as an Agent of Change: Communications and Cultural Transformations in Early Modern Europe*. Cambridge: Cambridge University Press, 1979.

———. *The Printing Revolution in Early Modern Europe*. Cambridge: Cambridge University Press, 1983.

Elias, Norbert. *The Court Society*. Translated by Edmund Jephcott. Oxford: Basil Blackwell, 1983.

Elsky, Martin. *Authorizing Words: Speech, Writing, and Print in the English Renaissance*. Ithaca, N.Y.: Cornell University Press, 1989.

Engelsing, Rolf. "Die Perioden der Lesegeschichte in der Neuzeit: Das statistische Ausmaß und die soziokulturelle Bedeutung der Lektüre." *Archiv für Geschichte des Buchwesens* 10 (1970): 945–1002.

Evans, Robert C. *Ben Jonson and the Poetics of Patronage*. Lewisburg, Penna.: Bucknell University Press, 1989.

Fabre, Daniel. *Écritures ordinaires*. Paris: P. O. L., 1994.

Febvre, Lucien and Henri-Jean Martin. *The Coming of the Book: The Impact of Printing 1450–1800*. Translated by David Gerard. London: Verso, 1984.

Foucault, Michel. "What Is an Author?" In *Textual Strategies: Perspectives in Post-Structural Criticism*, ed. Josué V. Harari, 141–60. Ithaca, N.Y.: Cornell University Press, 1979.

Foxon, David. *Pope and the Eighteenth-Century Book-Trade*. Edited and revised by James McLaverty. Lyell Lectures, 1975–1976. Oxford: Oxford University Press, 1991.

Gaines, James F. *Social Structures in Molière's Theater*, 148–55. Columbus: Ohio State University Press, 1984.

Ginzburg, Carlo. *The Cheese and the Worms: The Cosmos of a Sixteenth-Century Miller*. Translated by John Tedeschi and Anne Tedeschi. Baltimore: Johns Hopkins University Press, 1980.

Gold, Barbara K. *Literary Patronage in Greece and Rome*. Chapel Hill: University of North Carolina Press, 1987.

Goldmann, Lucien. *Essays on Method in the Sociology of Literature*. Saint Louis: Telos Press, 1980.

Goody, Jack. *The Domestication of the Savage Mind*. Cambridge: Cambridge University Press, 1977.

———. *The Logic of Writing and the Organization of Society*. Cambridge: Cambridge University Press, 1986.

———. *The Interface Between the Written and the Oral*. Cambridge: Cambridge University Press, 1987.

———, ed. *Literacy in Traditional Societies*. Cambridge: Cambridge University Press, 1968.

Gossman, Lionel. *Men and Masks: A Study of Molière*. Baltimore: Johns Hopkins University Press, 1963.

Greenblatt, Stephen. *Shakespearean Negotiations: The Circulation of Social Energy in Renaissance England*. Berkeley: University of California Press, 1988.

Grignon, Claude and Jean-Claude Passeron. *Le Savant et le populaire: Misérabilisme et populisme en sociologie et en littérature*. Paris: Gallimard Le Seuil, 1989.

Hall, David D. "The Uses of Literacy in New England, 1600–1850." In *Printing and Society in Early America*, ed. William L. Joyce, David D. Hall, R. D. Brown, and John B. Hench, 1–47. Worcester, Mass.: American Antiquarian Society, 1983.

———. *Worlds of Wonder, Days of Judgment: Popular Religious Belief in Early New England*. Cambridge, Mass.: Harvard University Press, 1989.

Harris, William V. *Ancient Literacy*. Cambridge, Mass.: Harvard University Press, 1989.

Havelock, Eric A. *The Muses Learn to Write: Reflections on Orality and Literacy from Antiquity to the Present*. New Haven, Conn.: Yale University Press, 1986.

Hesse, Carla. "Enlightenment Epistemology and Laws of Authorship in Revolutionary France, 1777–1793." *Representations* 30 (Spring 1990): 109–37.

Hindman, Sandra, ed. *Printing the Written Word: The Social History of Books, circa 1450–1520*. Ithaca, N.Y.: Cornell University Press, 1991.

Hoggart, Richard. *The Uses of Literacy: Aspects of Working-Class Life with Special Reference to Publications and Entertainments*. London: Chatto and Windus, 1957.

Holzknecht, Karl Julius. *Literary Patronage in the Middle Ages*. New York: Octagon Books, 1966.

Howarth, W. D. *Molière: A Playwright and His Audience*. Cambridge: Cambridge University Press, 1982.

Iser, Wolfgang. *The Act of Reading: A Theory of Aesthetic Response*. Baltimore: Johns Hopkins University Press, 1978.

Jardine, Lisa and Anthony Grafton. " 'Studied for Action': How Gabriel Harvey Read His Livy." *Past and Present* 129 (November 1990): 30–78.

Jauss, Hans Robert. *Aesthetic Experience and Literary Hermeneutics*. Translated by Michael Shaw. Minneapolis: University of Minnesota Press, 1982.

———. *Toward an Aesthetic of Reception*. Translated by Timothy Bahti. Minneapolis: University of Minnesota Press, 1982.

Jouhaud, Christian. "Histoire et histoire littéraire: Naissance de l'écrivain." *Annales E.S.C.* (1988): 849–66.

Kaplan, Steven L., ed. *Understanding Popular Culture: Europe from the Middle Ages to the Nineteenth Century*. Berlin: De Gruyter, 1984.

Kernan, Alvin. *Printing Technology, Letters, and Samuel Johnson*. Princeton, N.J.: Princeton University Press, 1987.

Knox, Bernard. "Silent Reading in Antiquity." *Greek, Roman, and Byzantine Studies* 9 (1968): 421–35.

Leiner, Wolfgang. *Der Widmungsbrief in der französischen Literatur (1580–1715)*. Heidelberg: Carl Winter Verlag, 1965.

Levine, Lawrence W. *Highbrow/Lowbrow: The Emergence of Cultural Hierarchy in America*. Cambridge, Mass.: Harvard University Press, 1988.

———. "The Folklore of Industrial Society: Popular Culture and Its Audience." *American Historical Review* 97, 5 (December 1992): 1369–89.

Lloyd, Geoffrey E. R. *Demystifying Mentalities*. Cambridge: Cambridge University Press, 1990.

Loewenstein, Joseph. "The Script in the Marketplace." *Representations* 12 (1985): 101–14.

Love, Harold. *Scribal Publication in Seventeenth-Century England*. Oxford: Oxford University Press, 1993.

Lyons, Martyn and Lucy Taksa. *Australian Readers Remember: An Oral History of Reading 1890–1930*. Melbourne: Oxford University Press, 1992.

Lytle, Guy Fitch and Stephen Orgel, eds. *Patronage in the Renaissance*. Princeton, N.J.: Princeton University Press, 1981.

McKenzie, D. F. *Bibliography and the Sociology of Texts*. The Panizzi Lectures, 1985. London: British Library, 1986.

———. "Typography and Meaning: The Case of William Congreve." In *Buch und Buchhandel in Europa im achtzehnten Jahrhundert*, ed. Giles Barber and Bernhard Fabian, 81–126. Hamburg: Hauswedell, 1981.

McKitterick, Rosamond. *The Carolingians and the Written Word*. Cambridge: Cambridge University Press, 1989.

Marco, Joaquín. *Literatura popular en España en los siglos XVIII y XIX (Una aproximación a los pliegos sueltos)*. Madrid: Taurus, 1977.

Martin, Henri-Jean, with Bruno Delmas. *Histoire et pouvoirs de l'écrit*. Paris: Librairie Académique Perrin, 1988.

Mortimer, Ruth. *A Portrait of the Author in Sixteenth-Century France*. The Hanes Foundation Lectures, I. Chapel Hill, N.C.: Hanes Foundation, 1980.

Moureau, François, ed. *De bonne main: La communication manuscrite au XVIIIe siècle*. Paris: Universitas, Oxford: Voltaire Foundation, 1993.

Mousnier, Roland and Jean Mesnard, eds. *L'Âge d'or du mécénat (1598–1661)*. Paris: Éditions du C.N.R.S., 1985.

Muchembled, Robert. *Popular Culture and Elite Culture in France, 1400–1750*. Translated by Lydia G. Cochrane. Baton Rouge: Louisiana State University Press, 1985.

Mukerji, Chandra and Michael Schudson, eds. *Rethinking Popular Culture: Contemporary Perspectives in Cultural Studies*. Berkeley: University of California Press, 1991.

Nelson, William. "From 'Listen, Lordings' to 'Dear Reader.'" *University of Toronto Quarterly: A Canadian Journal of the Humanities* 46, 2 (Winter 1976/77): 110–24.

Nies, Fritz. *Bahn und Bett und Blutenduft: Eine Reise durch die Welt der Leserbilder*. Darmstadt: Wissenschaftliche Buchgesellschaft, 1991.

Nunberg, Geoffrey. "The Places of Books in the Age of Electronic Reproduction." *Representations* 42 (Spring 1993): 13–37.

Ong, Walter. *Rhetoric, Romance, and Technology: Studies in the Interaction of Expression and Culture*. Ithaca, N.Y.: Cornell University Press, 1971.

———. *Interfaces of the Word: Studies in the Evolution of Consciousness and Culture*. Ithaca, N.Y.: Cornell University Press, 1977.

———. *Orality and Literacy: The Technologizing of the Word*. London and New York: Methuen, 1982.

Patterson, Annabel M. *Censorship and Interpretation: The Conditions of Writing and Reading in Early Modern England*. Madison: University of Wisconsin Press, 1984.

Peters, Julie Stone. *Congreve, the Drama, and the Printed Word*. Stanford, Calif.: Stanford University Press, 1990.

Petrucci, Armando. "Alle origini del libro moderno: libri da banco, libri da bisaccia, libretti da mano." In *Libri, scrittura e pubblico nel Rinascimento: Guida storica e critica*, ed. Armando Petrucci, 213–33. Rome and Bari: Laterza, 1979.

———. "Il libro manoscritto." In *Letteratura italiana*, 499–524. Produzione e consumo, vol. 2. Turin: Einaudi, 1983.

Radway, Janice A. *Reading the Romance: Women, Patriarchy, and Popular Literature*. Chapel Hill: University of North Carolina Press, 1984.

Ranum, Orest. *Artisans of Glory: Writers and Historical Thought in Seventeenth-Century France*. Chapel Hill: University of North Carolina Press, 1980.

———. "Islands and the Self in a Ludovician Fête." In *Sun King: The Ascendancy of French Culture during the Reign of Louis XIV*, ed. David Lee Rubin, 17–34. Washington, D.C.: Folger Library; London and Toronto: Associated University Presses, 1992.

Rico, Francisco. "La *princeps* del *Lazarillo*: Título, capitulación y epígrafes de un texto apócrifo." In *Problemas del Lazarillo*, ed. Francisco Rico, 113–51. Madrid: Cátedra, 1988.

Roberts, Colin H. and T. C. Skeat. *The Birth of the Codex*. London and New York: Oxford University Press, 1983.

Rose, Mark. *Authors and Owners: The Invention of Copyright*. Cambridge, Mass.: Harvard University Press, 1993.

Rossi, Pietro, ed. *La memoria del sapere: Forme di conservazione e strutture organizzative dell'Antichità a oggi*. Rome and Bari: Laterza, 1988.

Saenger, Paul. "Silent Reading: Its Impact on Late Medieval Script and Society." *Viator: Medieval and Renaissance Studies* 13 (1982): 367–414.

———. "The Separation of Words and the Order of Words: The Genesis of Medieval Reading." *Scrittura e Civiltà* 14 (1990): 49–74.

Scheid, John and Jesper Svenbro. *Le métier de Zeus: Mythe du tissage et du tissu dans le monde gréco-romain*. Paris: Éditions la Découverte, 1994.

Schön, Erich. *Der Verlust der Sinnlichkeit oder die Verwandlungen des Lesers: Mentalitätswandel um 1800*. Stuttgart: Klett-Cotta, 1987.

Schöttenloher, Karl. *Die Widmungsvorrede im Buch des 16. Jahrhunderts*. Munich: Aschendorff, 1953.

Shapin, Steven. "'The Mind in Its Own Place': Science and Solitude in Seventeenth-Century England." *Science in Context* 4, 1 (1990): 192–217.

Spufford, Margaret. *Small Books and Pleasant Histories: Popular Fiction and Its Readership in Seventeenth-Century England*. London: Methuen, 1981.

Stock, Brian. *The Implications of Literacy: Written Language and Models of Interpretation in the Eleventh and Twelfth Centuries*. Princeton, N.J.: Princeton University Press, 1983.

Stoddard, Roger. "Morphology and the Book from an American Perspective." *Printing History* 17 (1990): 2–14.

Svenbro, Jesper. *Phrasikleia: Anthropologie de la lecture en Grèce ancienne*. Paris: Éditions La Découverte, 1988.

Tanselle, G. Thomas. "The Latest Forms of Book-Burning." *Common Knowledge* 2, 3 (Winter 1993): 172–77.

Teyssèdre, Bernard. *L'Art français au siècle de Louis XIV*. Paris: Le Livre de Poche, 1967.

Trapp, J. B., ed. *Manuscripts in the Fifty Years after the Invention of Printing: Some Papers Read at a Colloquium at the Warburg Institute on 12–13 March 1982*. London: Warburg Institute, University of London, 1983.

Veeser, H. Aram, ed. *The New Historicism*. New York and London: Routledge, 1989.

Velay-Vallantin, Catherine. *L'Histoire des contes*. Paris: Fayard, 1992.

Viala, Alain. *Naissance de l'écrivain: Sociologie de la littérature à l'âge classique*. Paris: Éditions de Minuit, 1985.

Warnke, Martin. *The Court Artist: On the Ancestry of the Modern Artist*. Translated by David McLintock. Cambridge: Cambridge University Press, 1992.

Watt, Tessa. *Cheap Print and Popular Piety, 1550–1640*. Cambridge: Cambridge University Press, 1991.

Woodmansee, Martha. "The Genius and the Copyright: Economic and Legal Conditions of the Emergence of the Author." *Eighteenth-Century Studies* 17, 4 (1984): 51–85.

Woodmansee, Martha and Peter Jaszi, eds. *The Construction of Authorship: Textual Appropriation in Law and Literature*. Durham, N.C.: Duke University Press, 1994.

Zanger, Abby. "Paralyzing Performance: Sacrificing the Theater on the Altar of Publication." *Stanford French Review* (1988): 169–85.

Zammito, John H. "Are We Being Theoretical Yet? The New Historicism, the New Philosophy of History, and 'Practicing History.'" *The Journal of Modern History* 65, 4 (December 1993): 783–814.

Zapperi, Roberto. *Annibale Carraci: Ritratto di artista da giovane*. Turin: Einaudi, 1989.

Zedelmaier, Helmut. *Bibliotheca Universalis und Bibliotheca Selecta: Das Problem der Ordnung des gelehrten Wissens in der frühen Neuzeit*. Cologne, Weimar, and Vienna: Böhlau Verlag, 1992.

Index

University of Pennsylvania Press
NEW CULTURAL STUDIES
Joan DeJean, Carroll Smith-Rosenberg,
and Peter Stallybrass, Editors

Jonathan Arac and Harriet Ritvo, editors. *Macropolitics of Nineteenth-Century Literature: Nationalism, Exoticism, Imperialism*. 1991

John Barrell. *The Birth of Pandora and the Division of Knowledge*. 1992

Bruce Thomas Boehrer. *Monarchy and Incest in Renaissance England: Literature, Culture, Kinship, and Kingship*. 1992

Carol Breckenridge and Peter van der Veer, editors. *Orientalism and the Postcolonial Predicament: Perspectives on South Asia*. 1993

E. Jane Burns. *Bodytalk: When Women Speak in Old French Literature*. 1993

Roger Chartier. *Forms and Meanings: Texts, Performances, and Audiences from Codex to Computer*. 1995

Joseph W. Childers. *Novel Possibilities: Fiction and the Formation of Earl, Victorian Culture*. 1995

Richard Dellamora. *Postmodern Apocalypse: Theory and Cultural Practice at the End*. 1995

Jones DeRitter. *The Embodiment of Characters: The Representation of Physical Experience on Stage and in Print, 1728–1749*. 1994

Julia V. Douthwaite. *Exotic Women: Literary Heroines and Cultural Strategies in Ancien Régime France*. 1992

Barbara J. Eckstein. *The Language of Fiction in a World of Pain: Reading Politics as Paradox*. 1990

Jean Marie Goulemot. (James Simpson, trans.) *Forbidden Texts: Erotic Literature and Its Readers in Eighteenth-Century France*. 1995

Kathryn Gravdal. *Ravishing Maidens: Writing Rape in Medieval French Literature and Law*. 1991

Deborah A. Kapchan. *Gender on the Market: Revoicing Tradition in Beni Mellal, Morocco*. 1996

Jayne Ann Krentz, editor. *Dangerous Men and Adventurous Women: Romance Writers on the Appeal of the Romance*. 1992

Carole Levin. *The Heart and Stomach of a King: Elizabeth I and the Politics of Sex and Power*. 1994

Linda Lomperis and Sarah Stanbury, editors. *Feminist Approaches to the Body in Medieval Literature*. 1993

Karma Lochrie. *Margery Kempe and Translations of the Flesh*. 1991

Alex Owen. *The Darkened Room: Women, Power and Spiritualism in Late Victorian England*. 1990

Jacqueline Rose. *The Case of Peter Pan or The Impossibility of Children's Fiction*. 1992

Alan Sinfield. *Cultural Politics — Queer Reading*. 1994

This book has been set in Linotron Galliard. Galliard was designed for Mergenthaler in 1978 by Matthew Carter. Galliard retains many of the features of a sixteenth-century typeface cut by Robert Granjon but has some modifications that give it a more contemporary look.

Printed on acid-free paper.